Fairydust

Enchanting Fairy Coloring Book

artwork by

Lillian Asterios

Sketch Page

A glass of absinthe is poetical as anything in the world. What difference is there between a glass of absinthe and a sunset?

Oscar Wilde

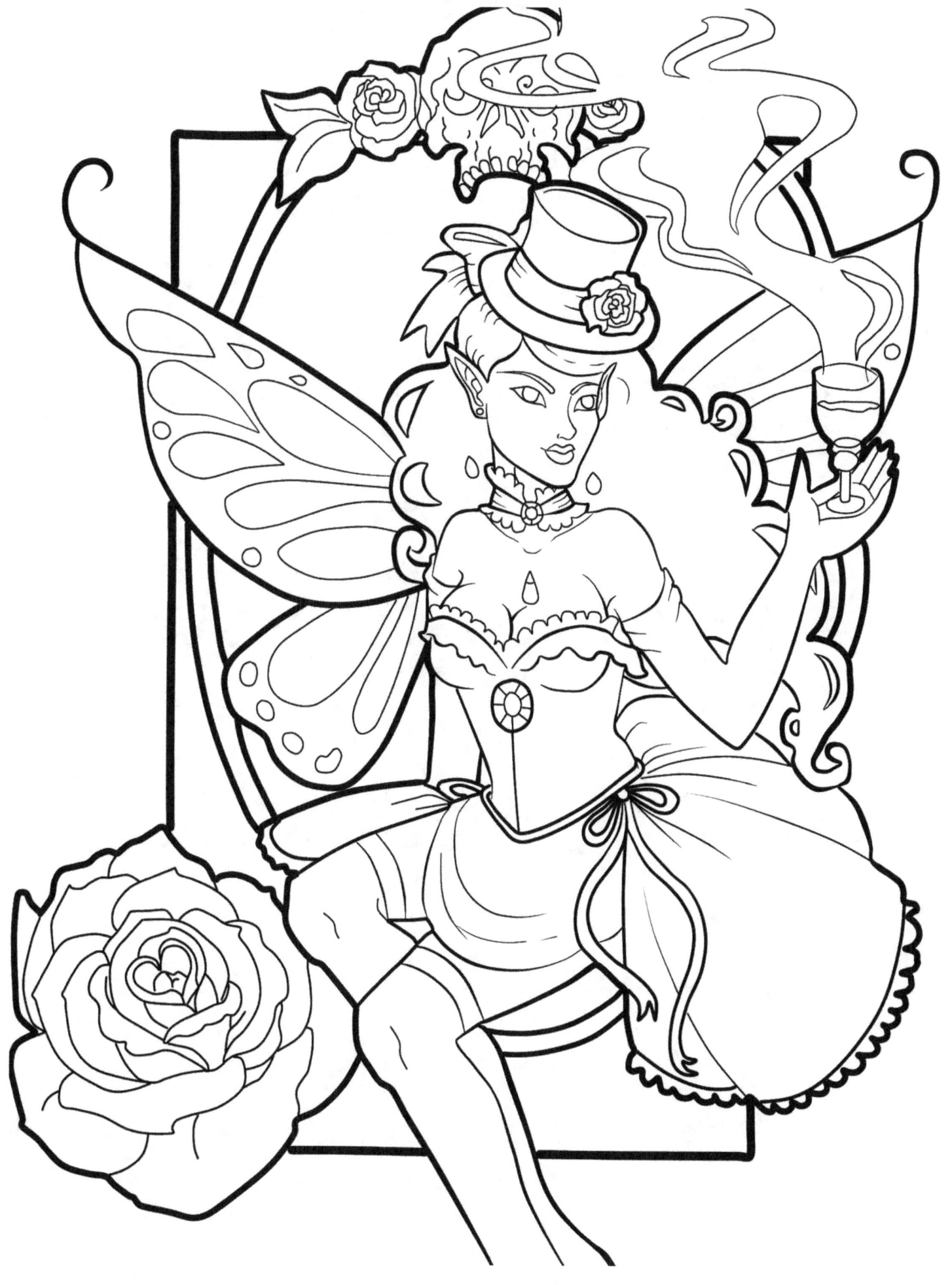

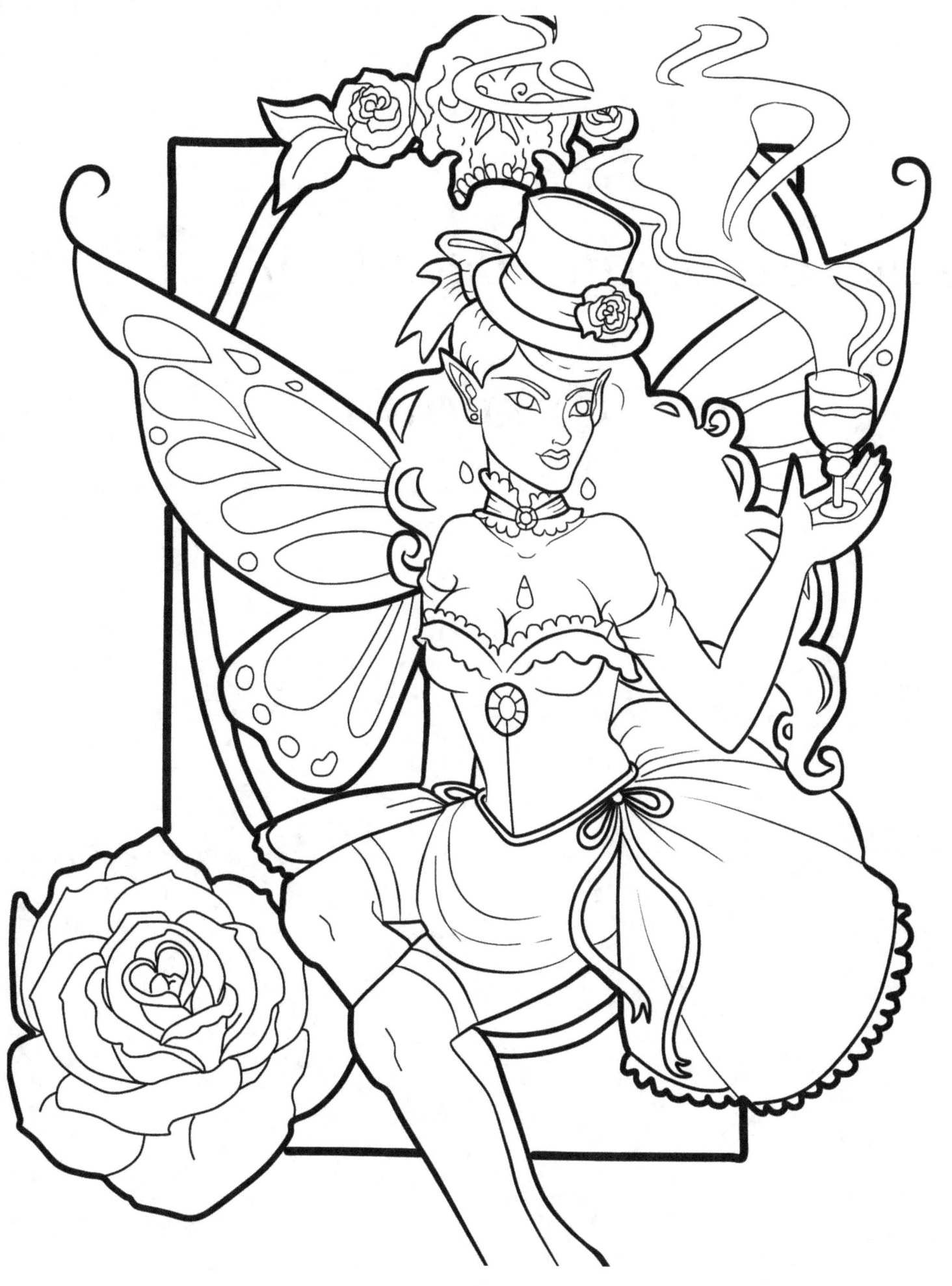

You're a bright, beautiful goddess.

Unknown

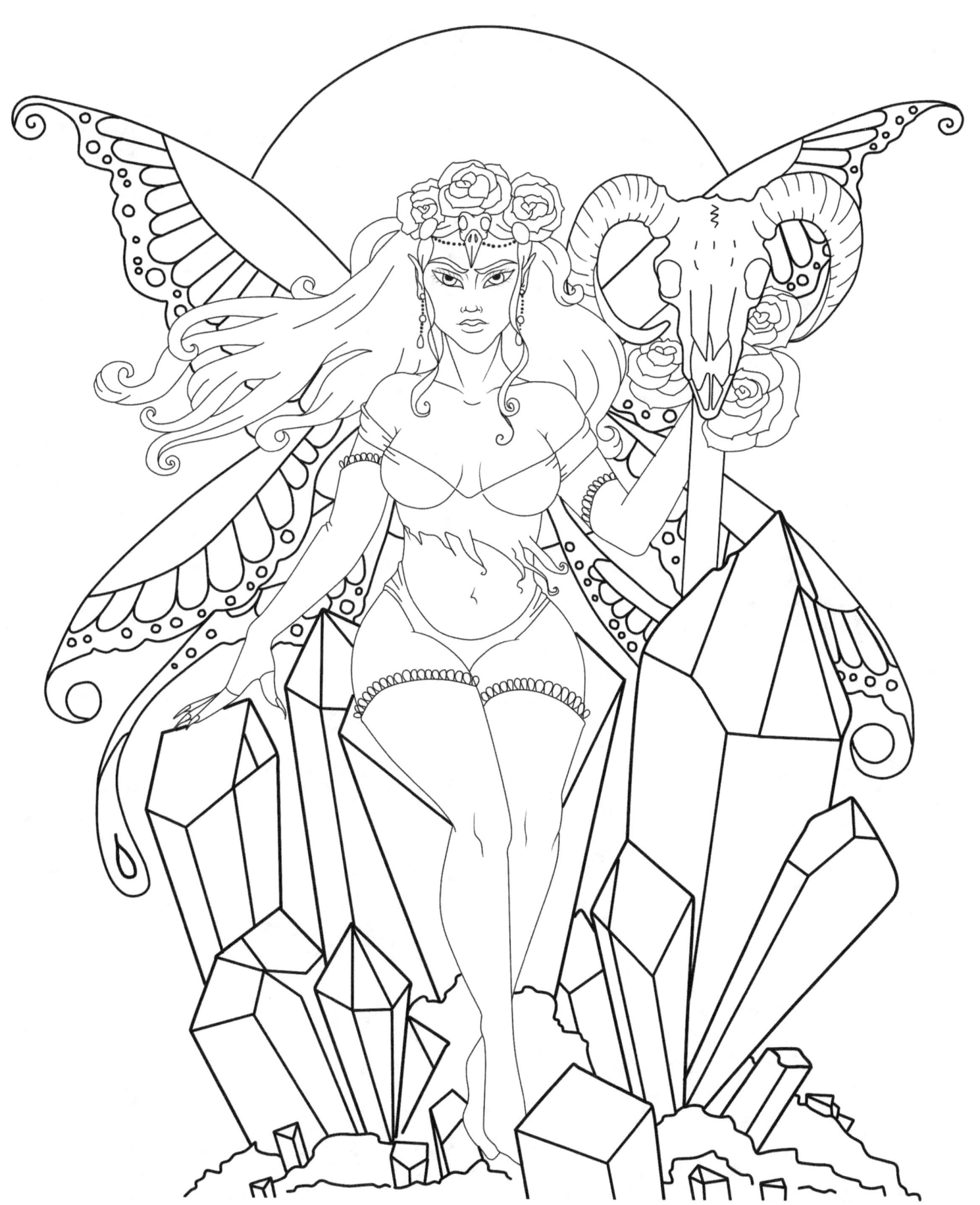

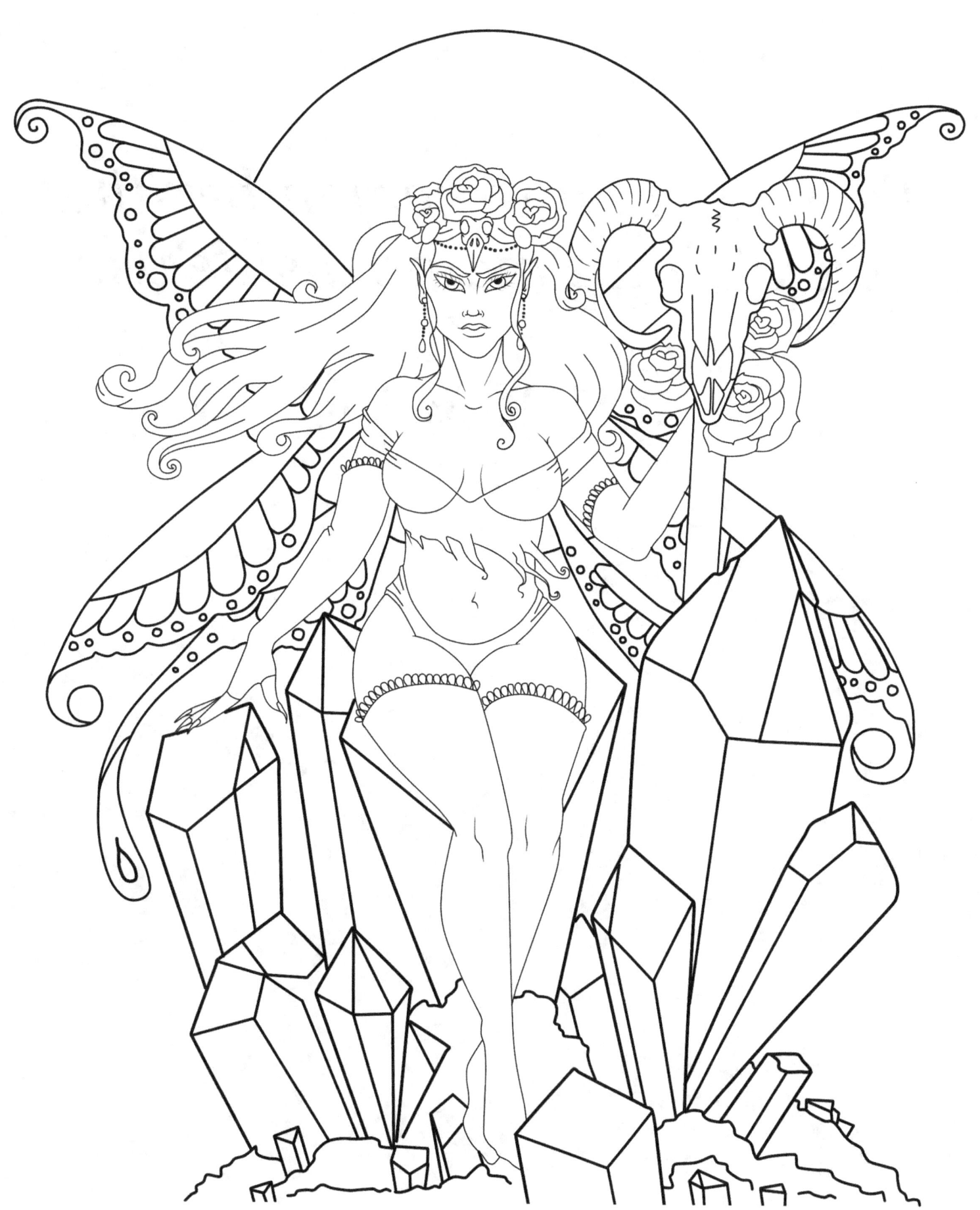

It's important to remember that we all have magic inside us.

J.K. Rowling

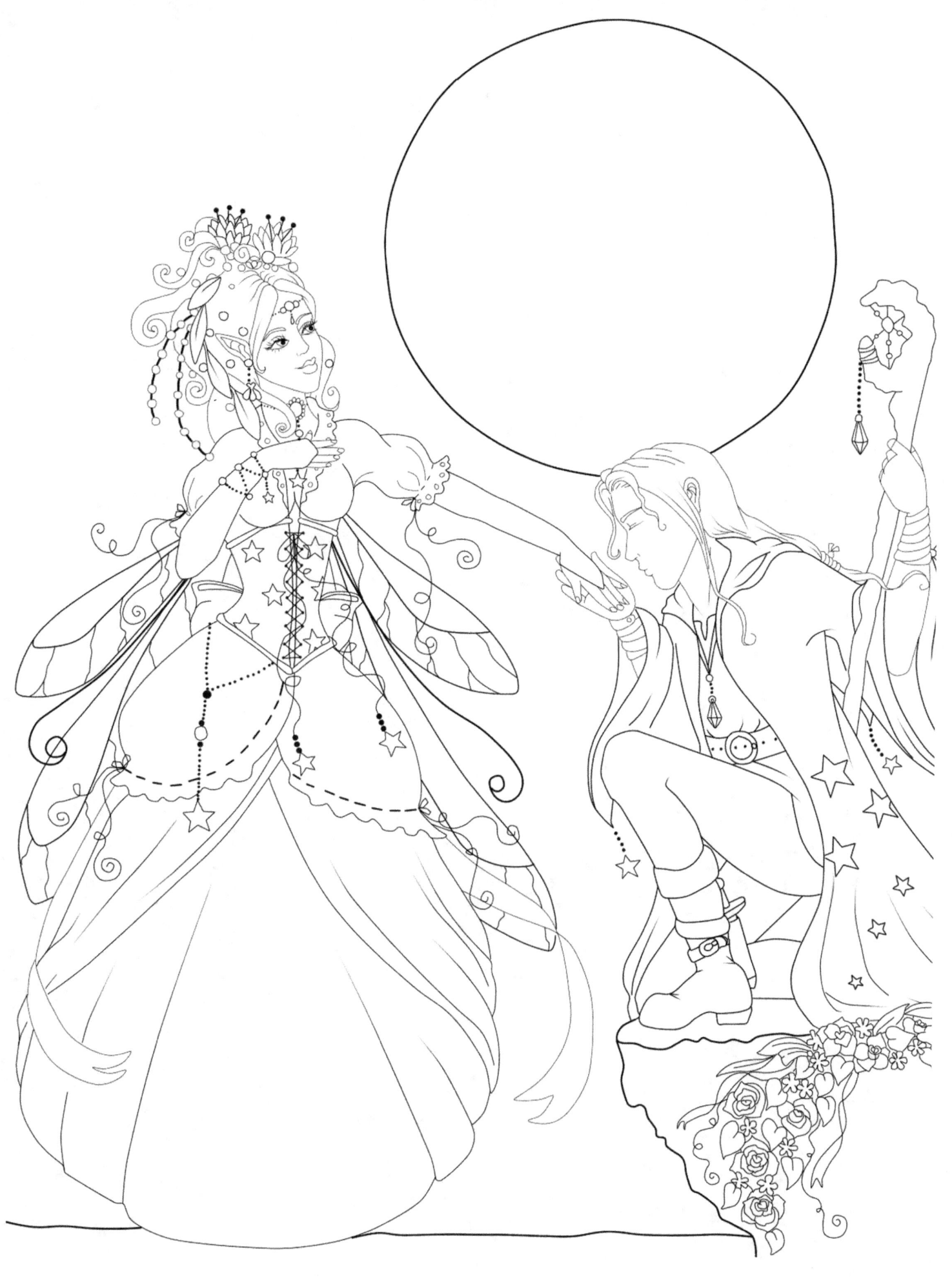

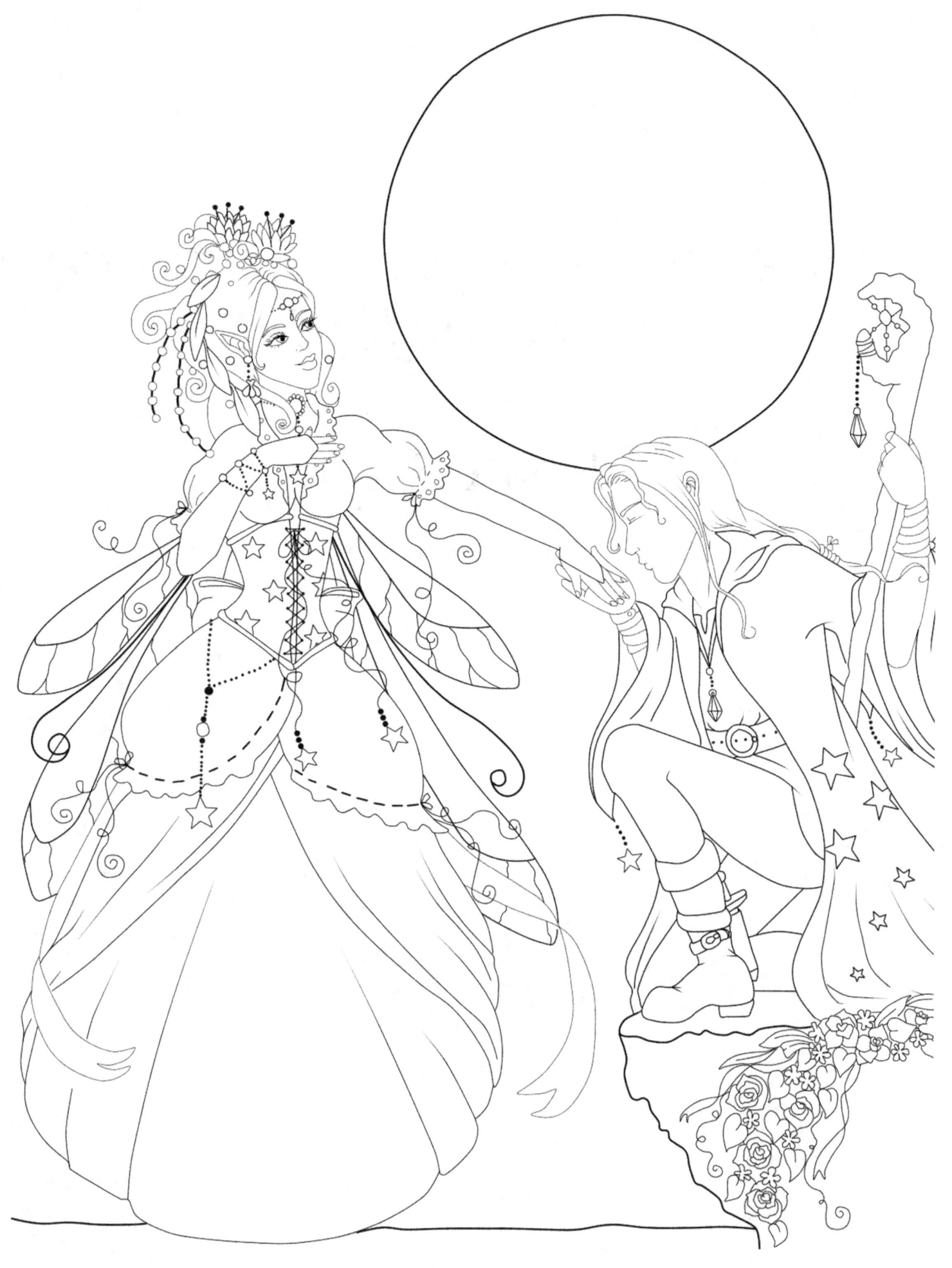

*Those who don't believe in magic
will never find it.*

Roald Dahl

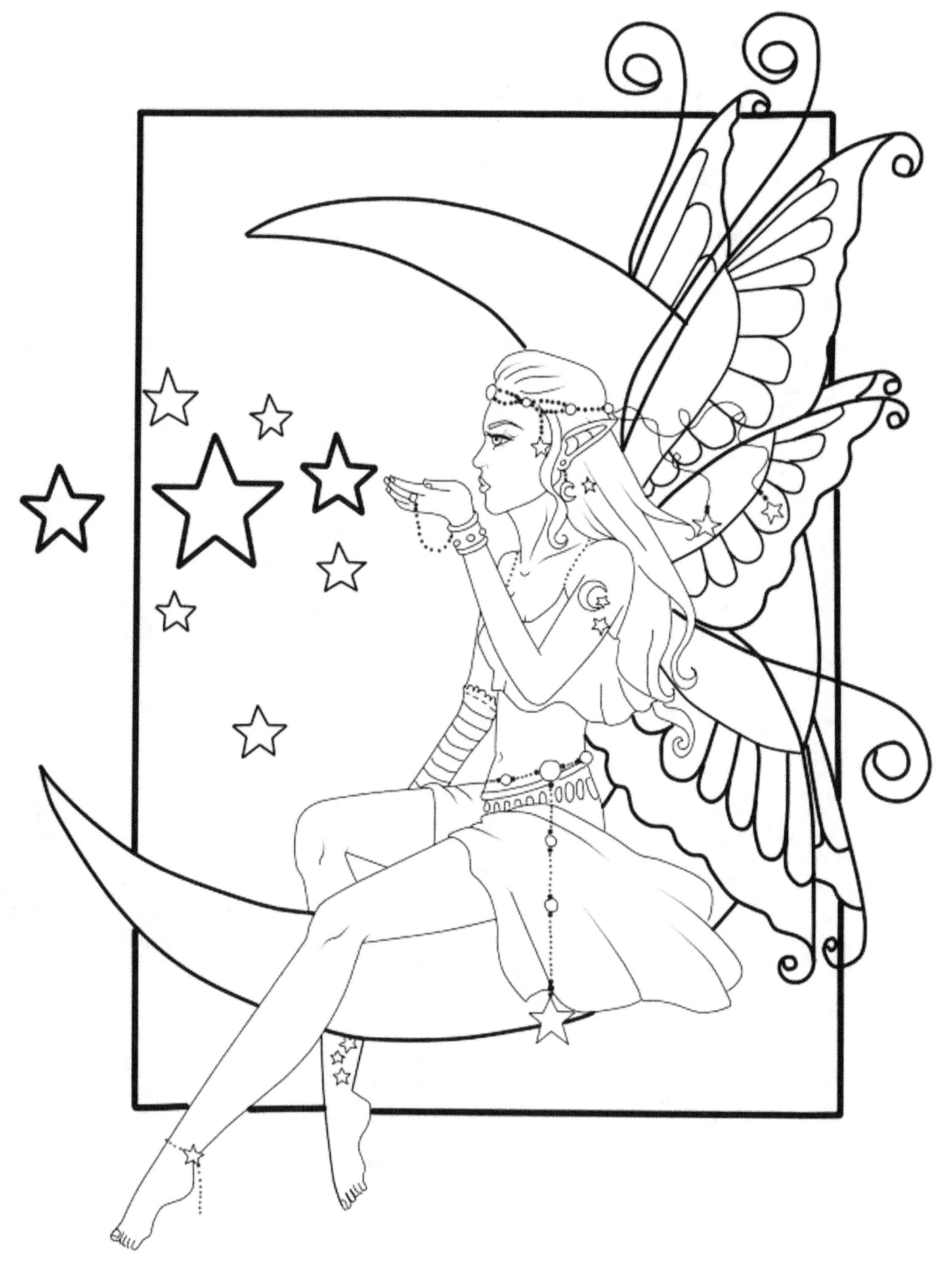

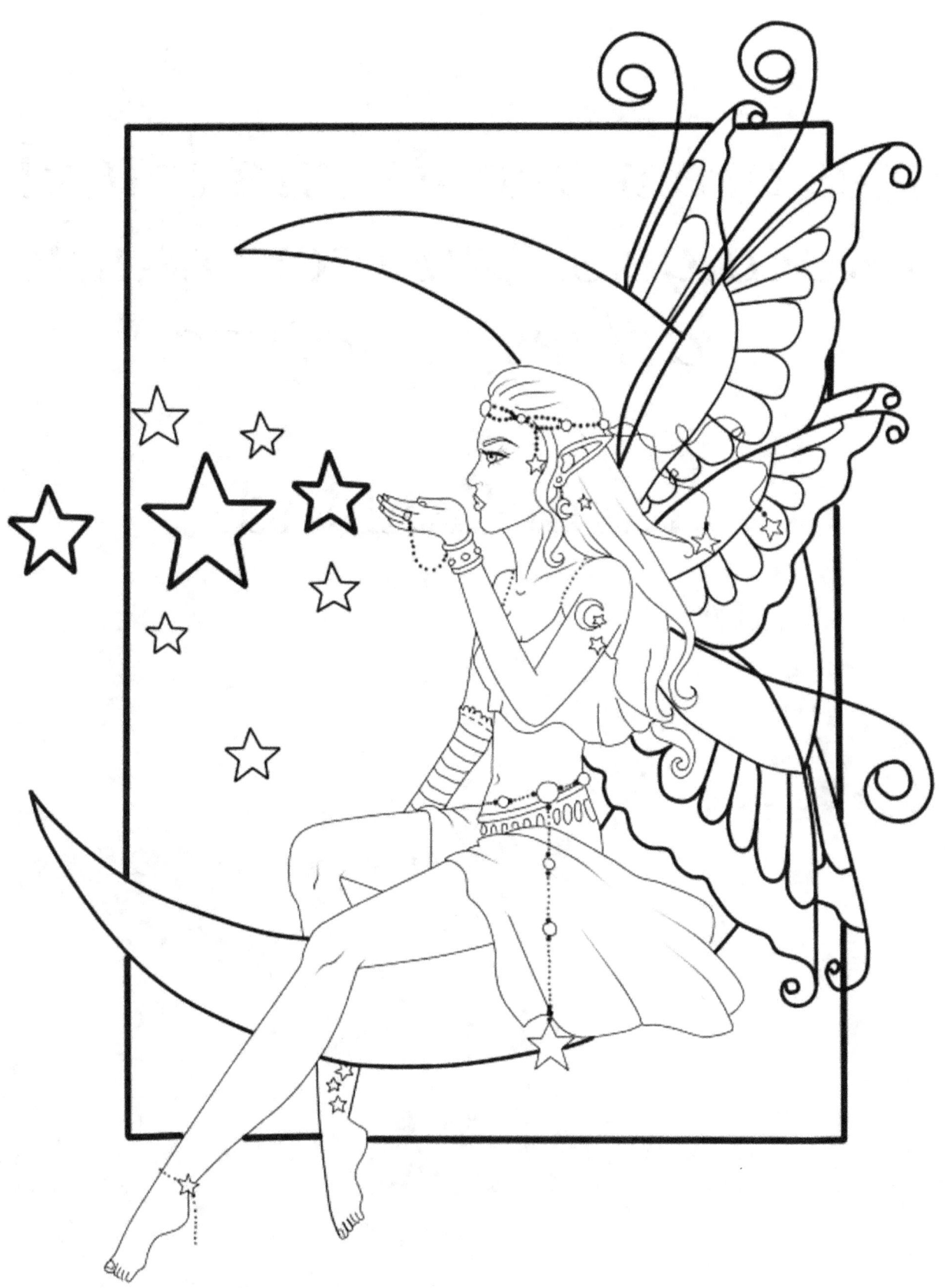

Fairies are invisible and inaudible like angels. But their magic sparkles in nature.

Lynn Holland

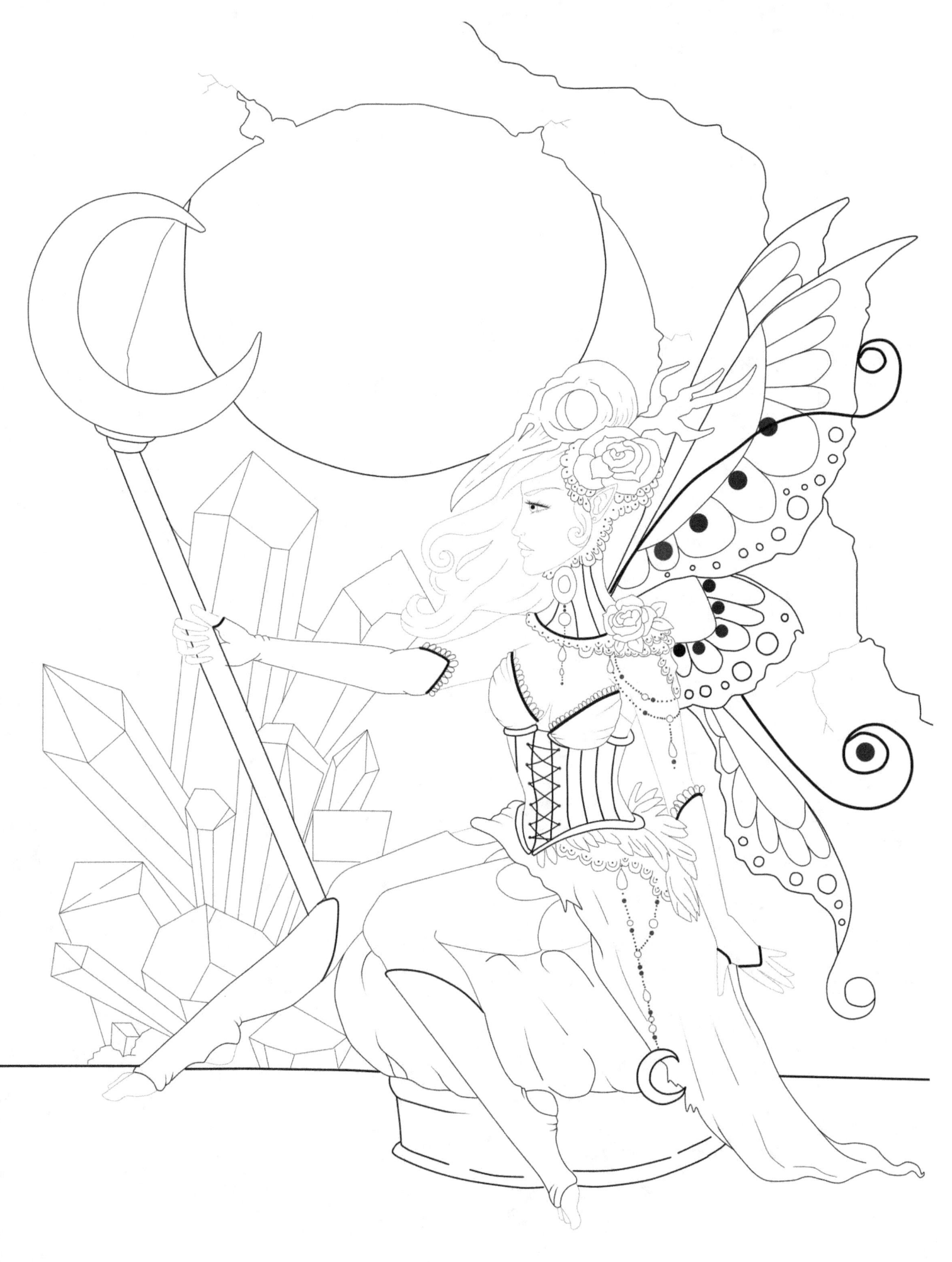

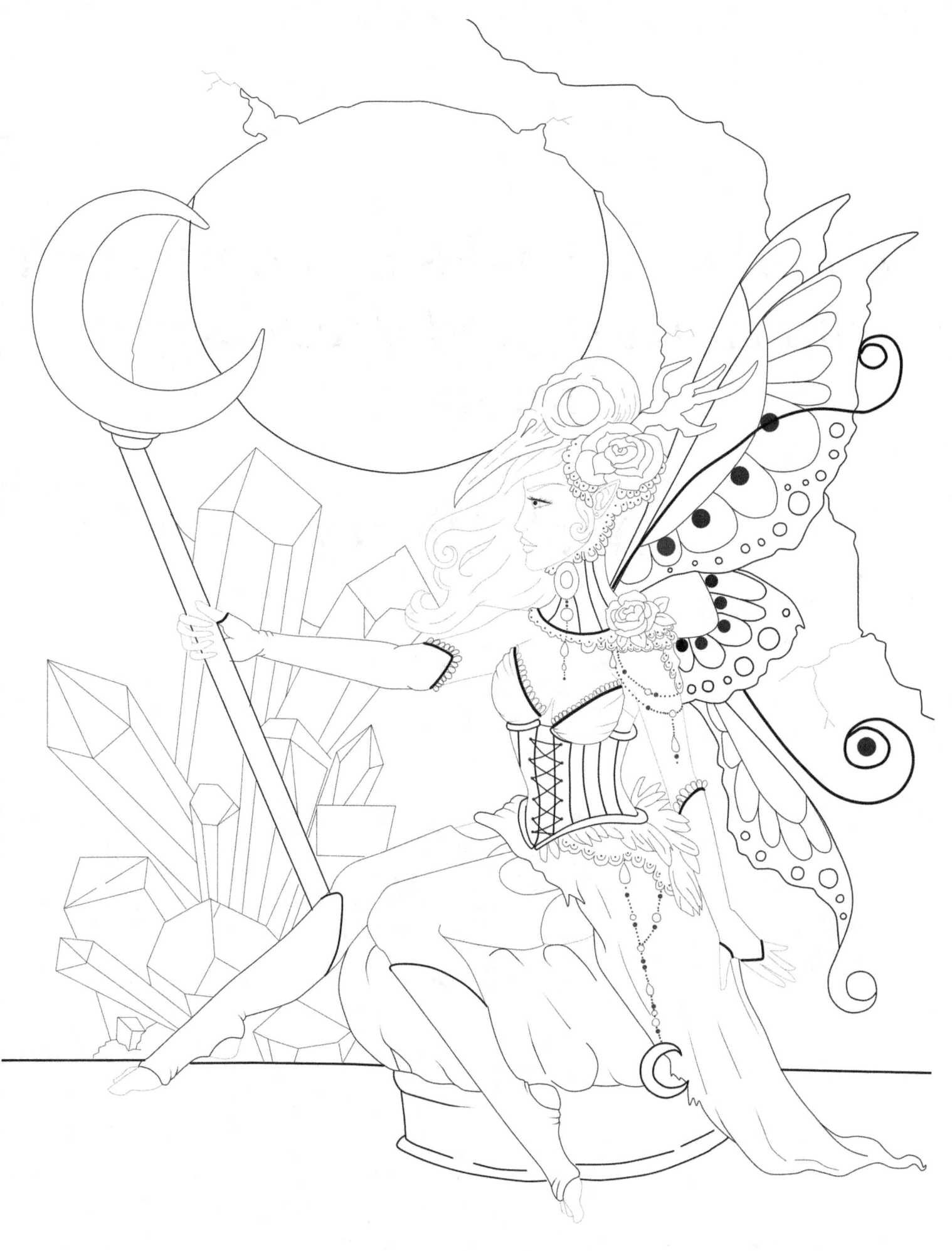

Laughter is timeless, imagination has no age, and dreams are forever.

Walt Disney

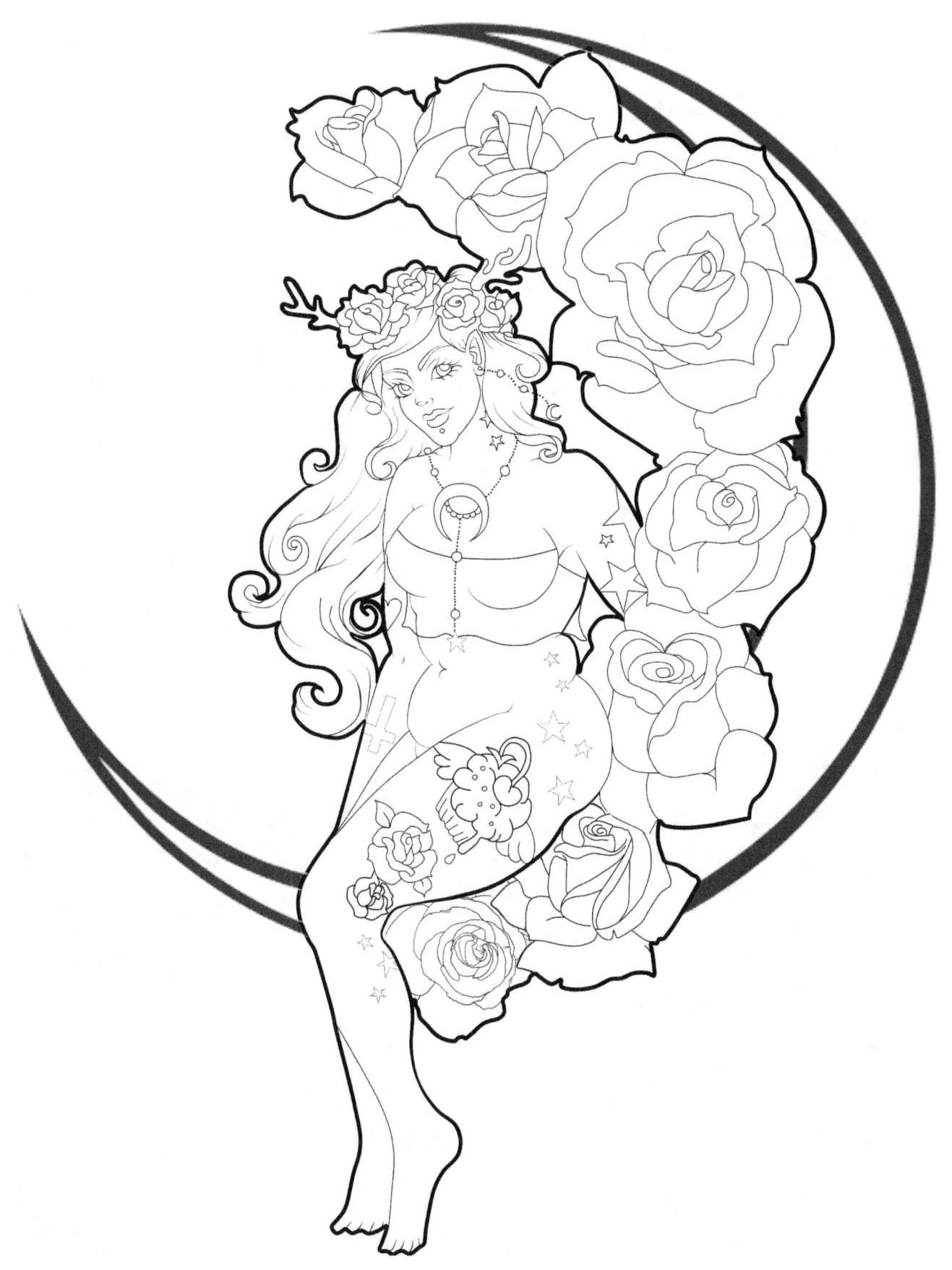

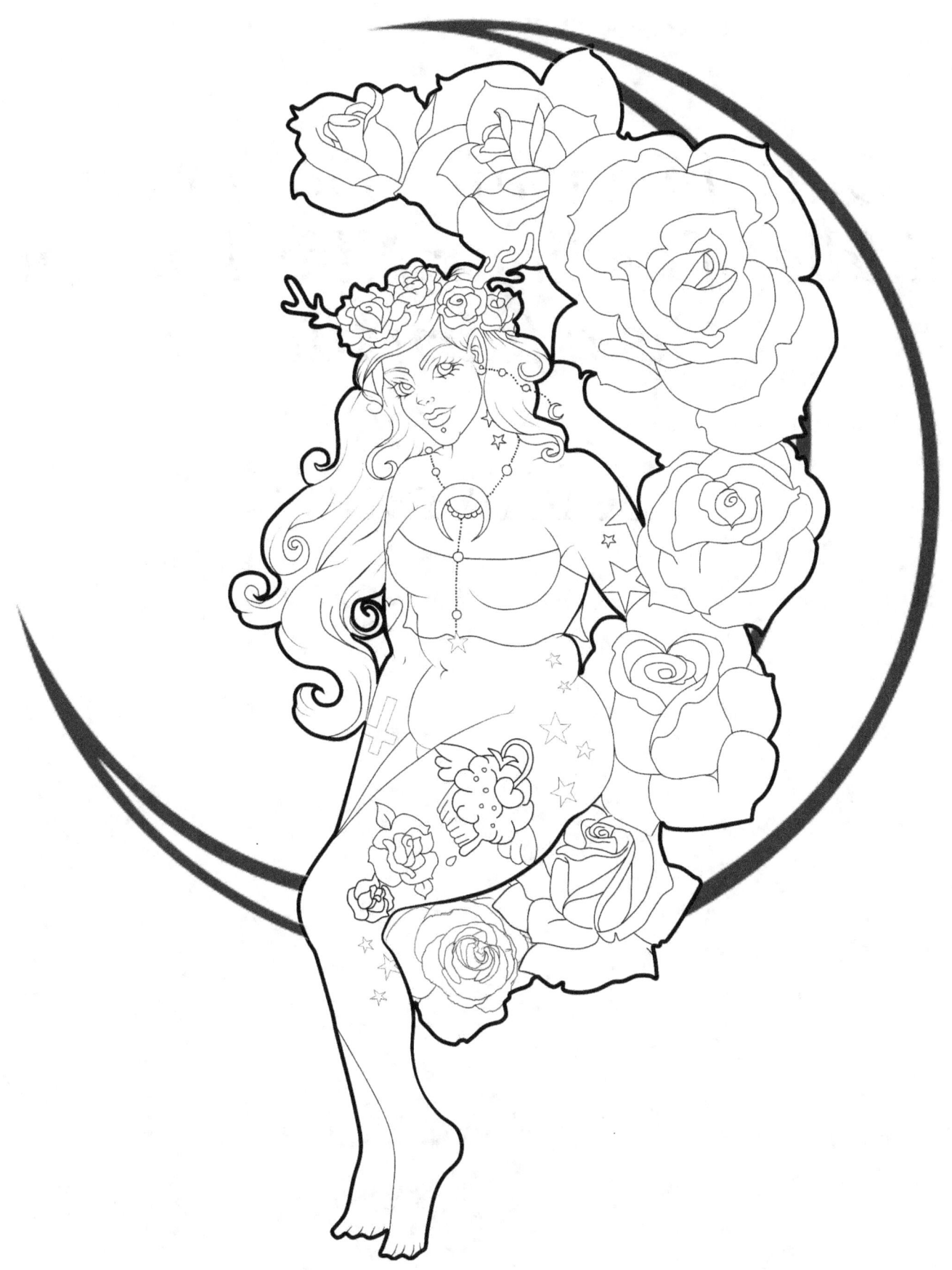

Once in a while, right in the middle of ordinary life, love gives us a fairy tale.

Anonymous

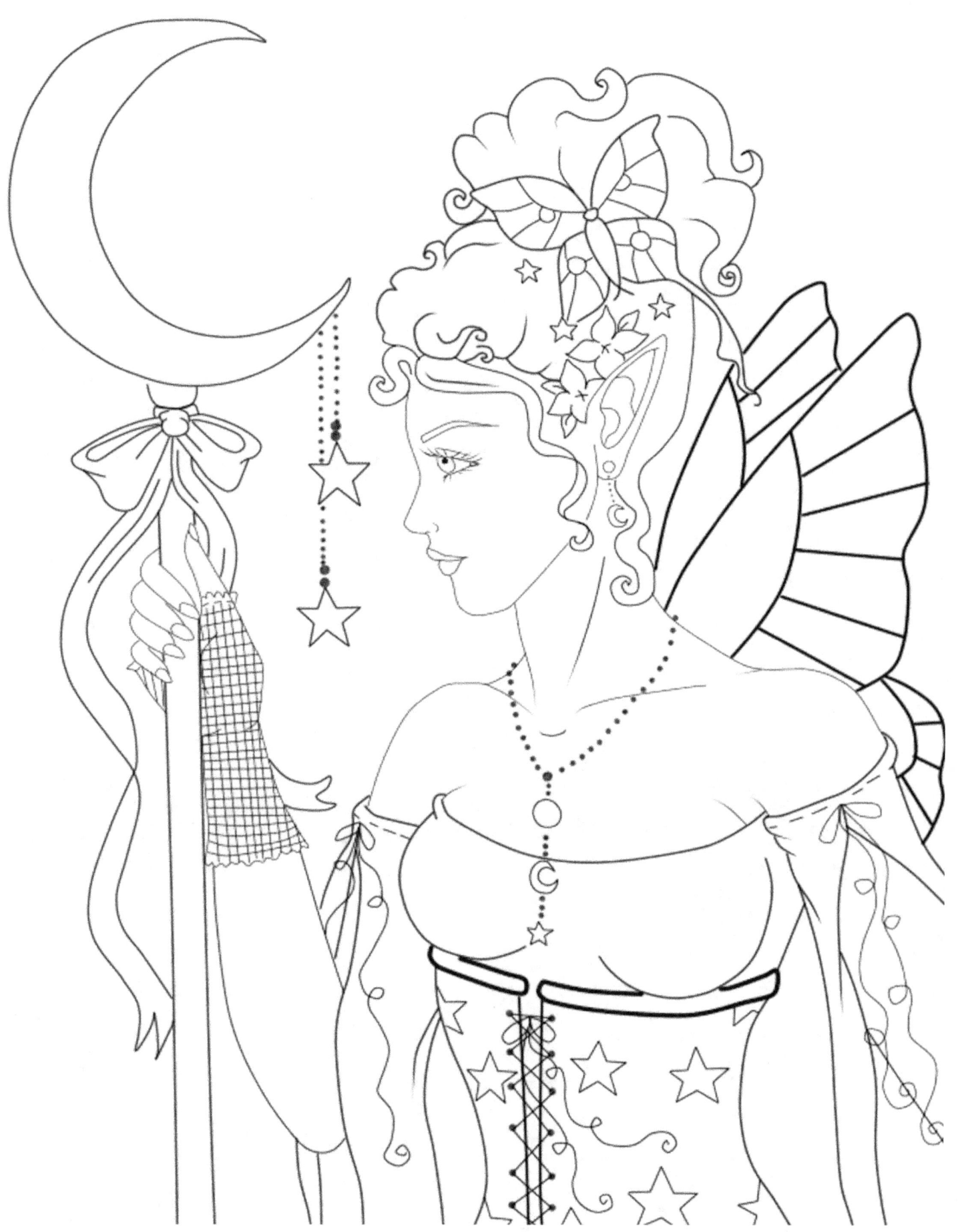

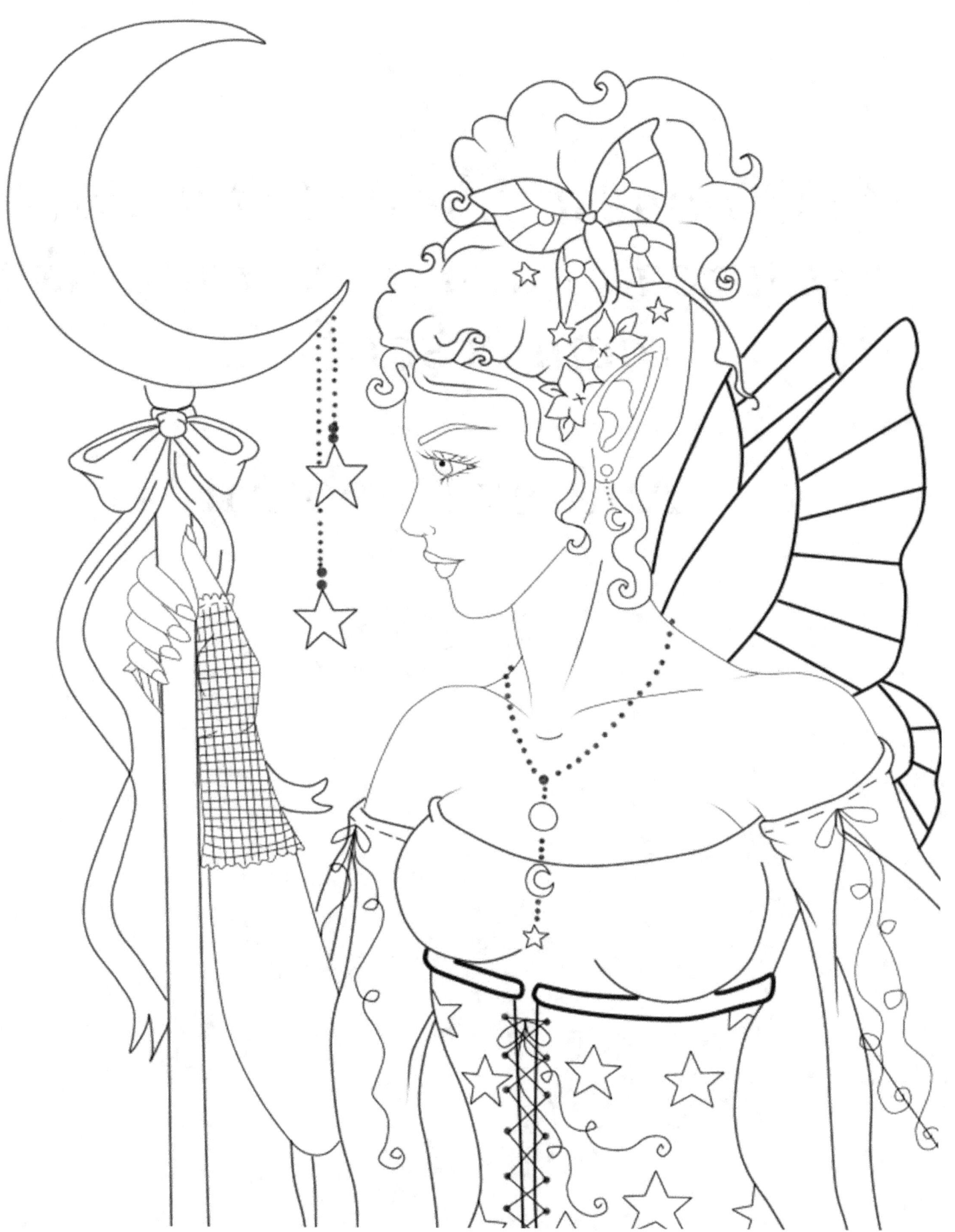

If I'm honest, I have to tell you...
I still read fairy tales and I like
them best of all.

Audrey Hepburn

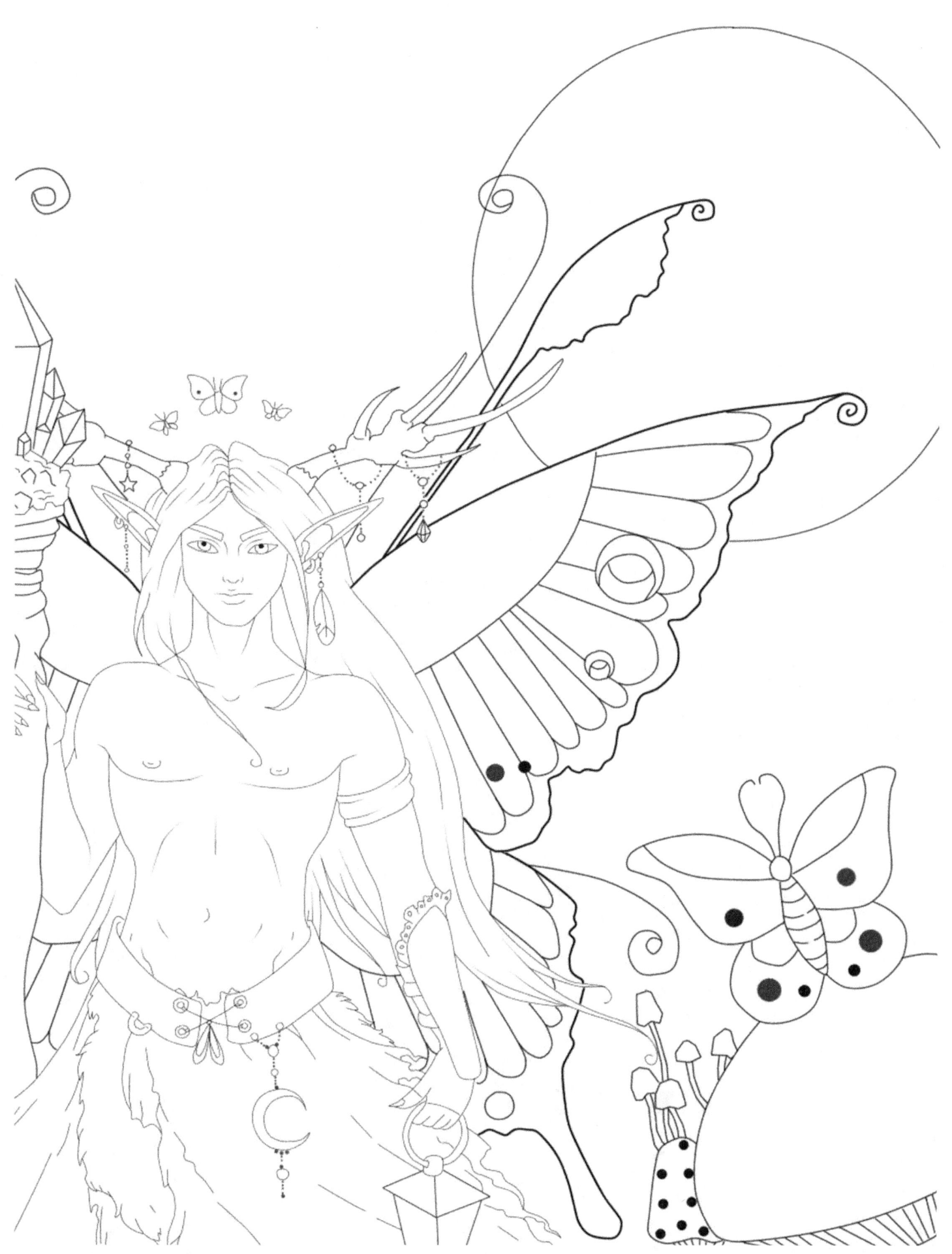

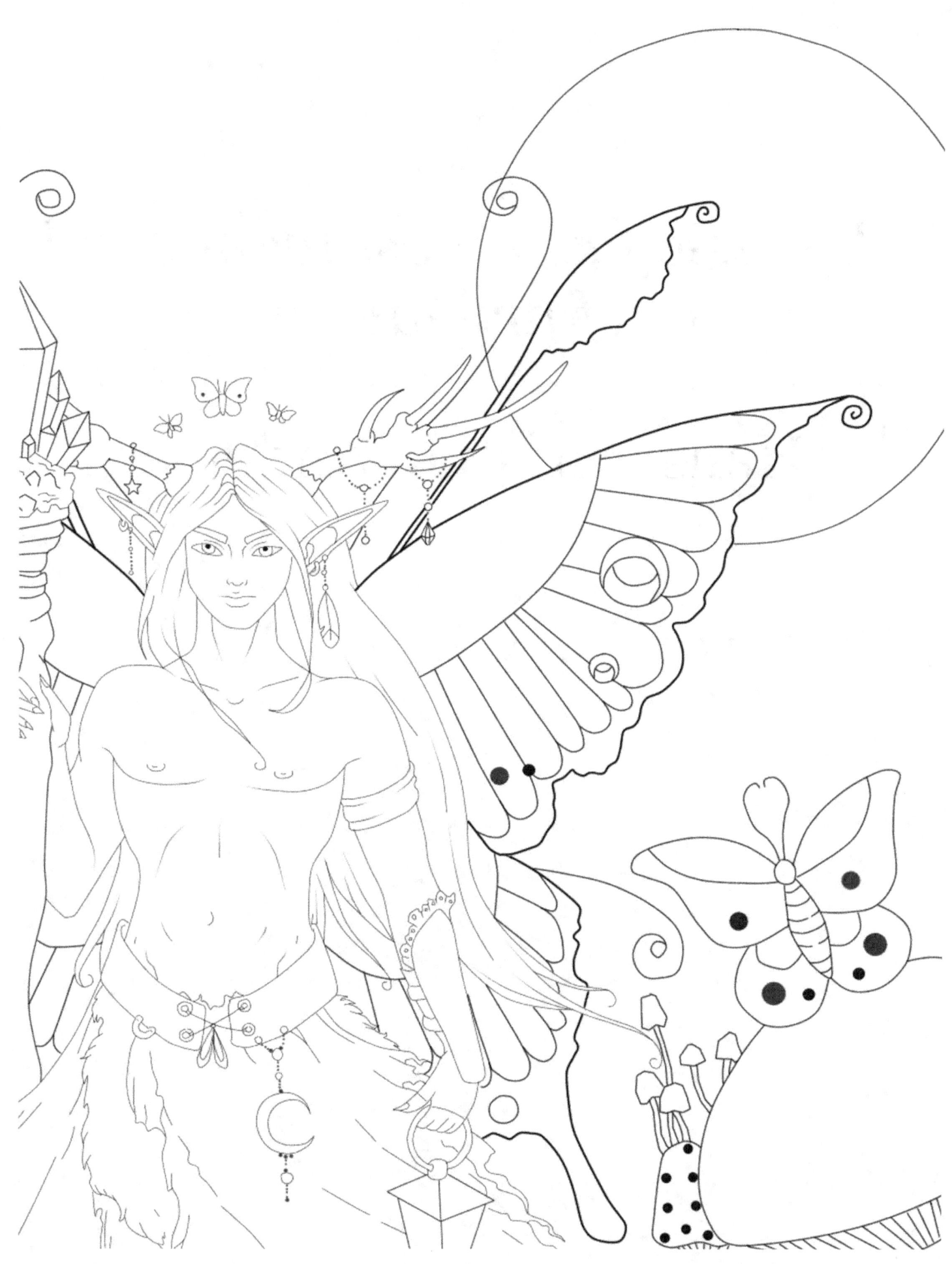

Life itself is a most wonderful fairy tale.

Hans Christian Andersen

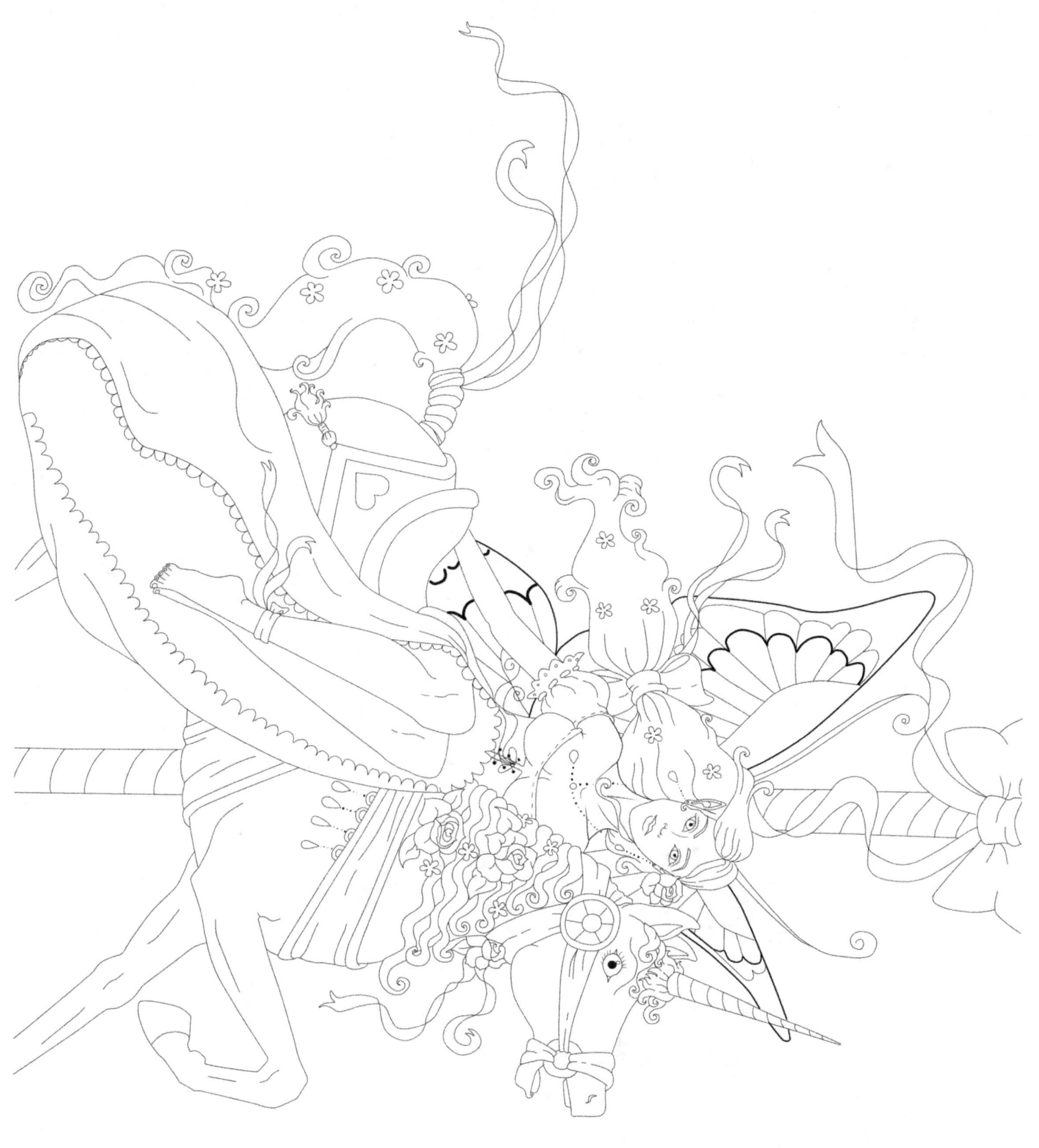

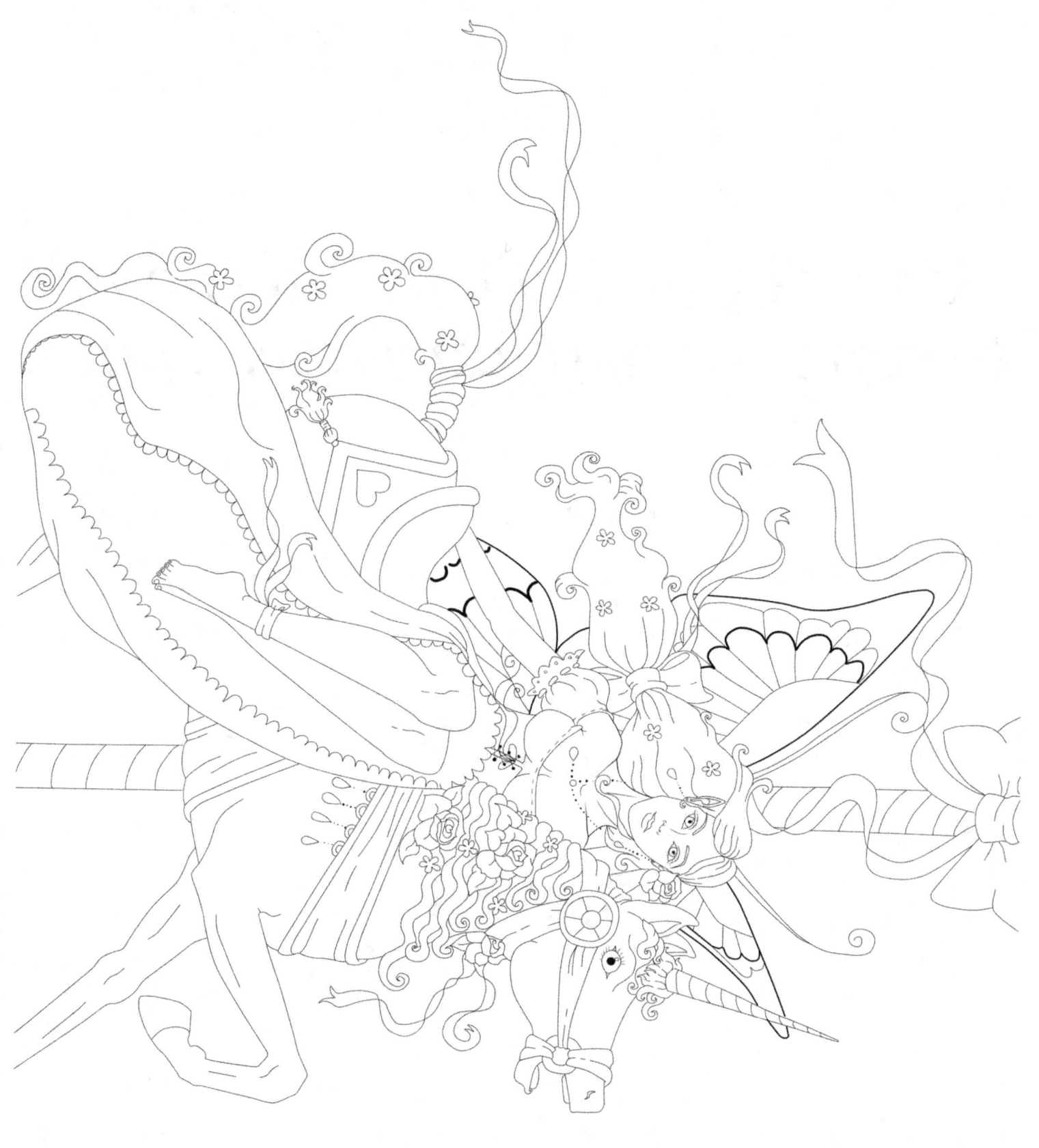

Some day you will be old enough to start reading fairy tales again.

C.S. Lewis

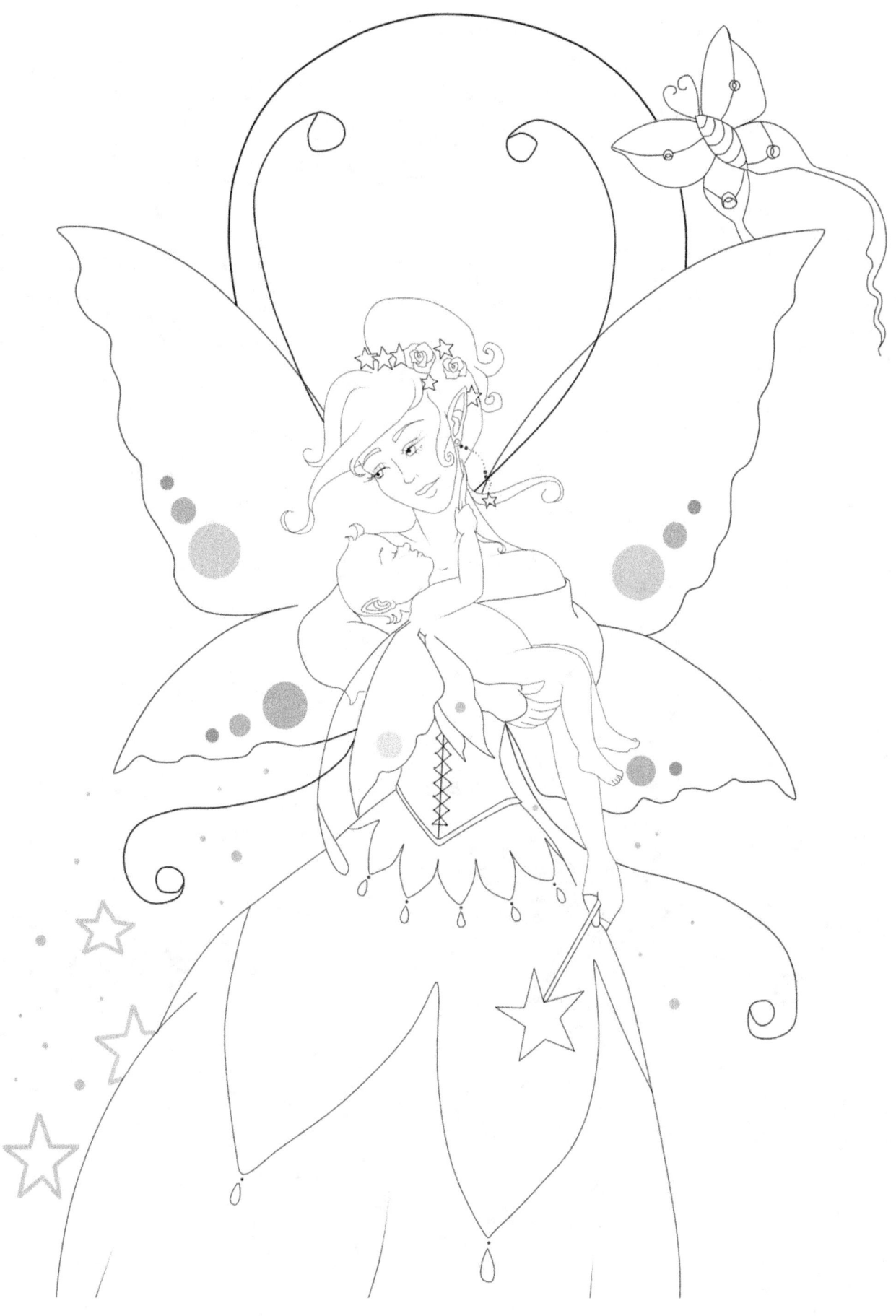

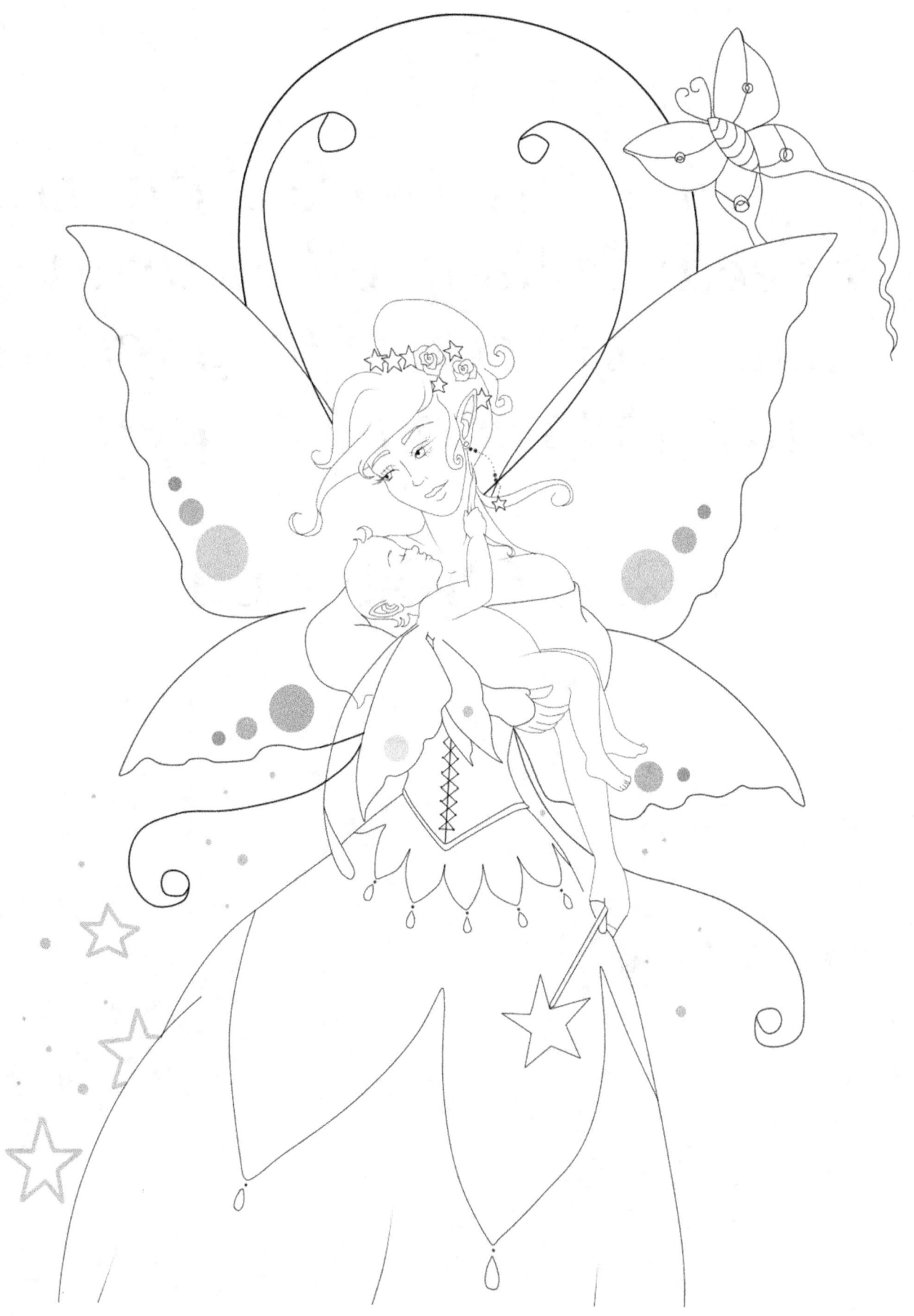

*Fairy tales are more than true;
not because they tell us dragons
exist, but because they tell us
dragons can be beaten.*

G.K. Chesterton

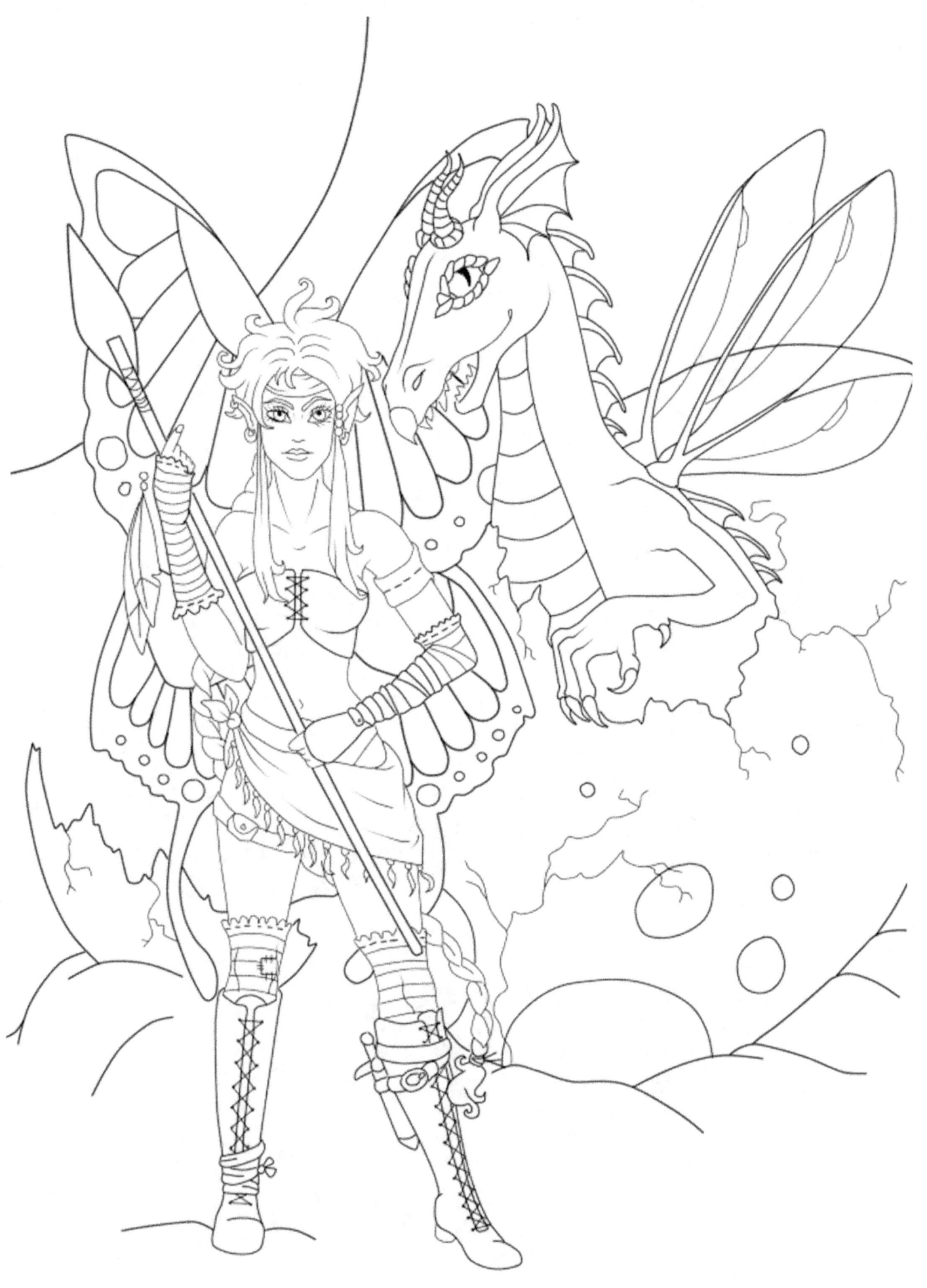

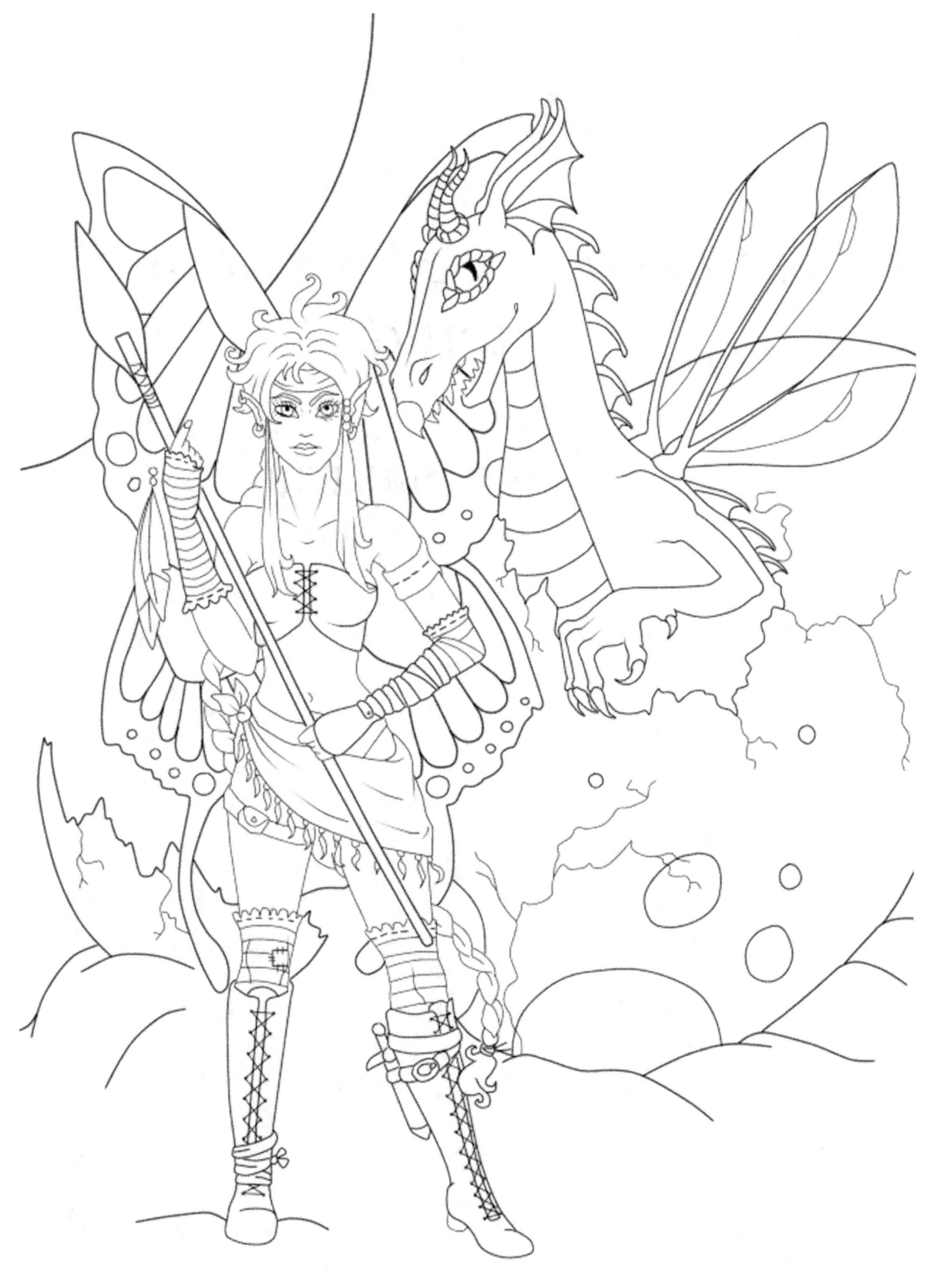

Any man can lose his hat in a fairy wind.

Irish Saying

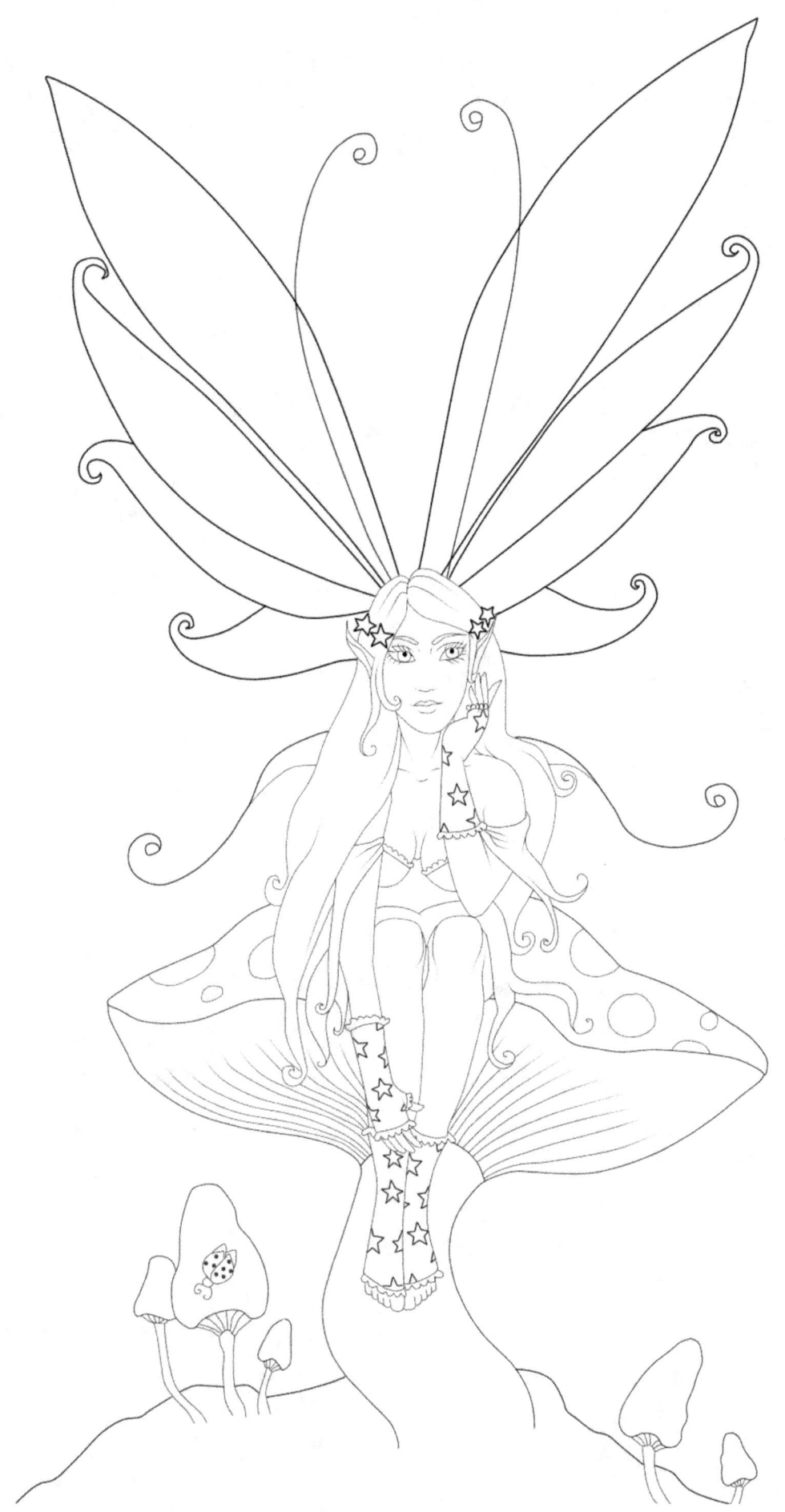

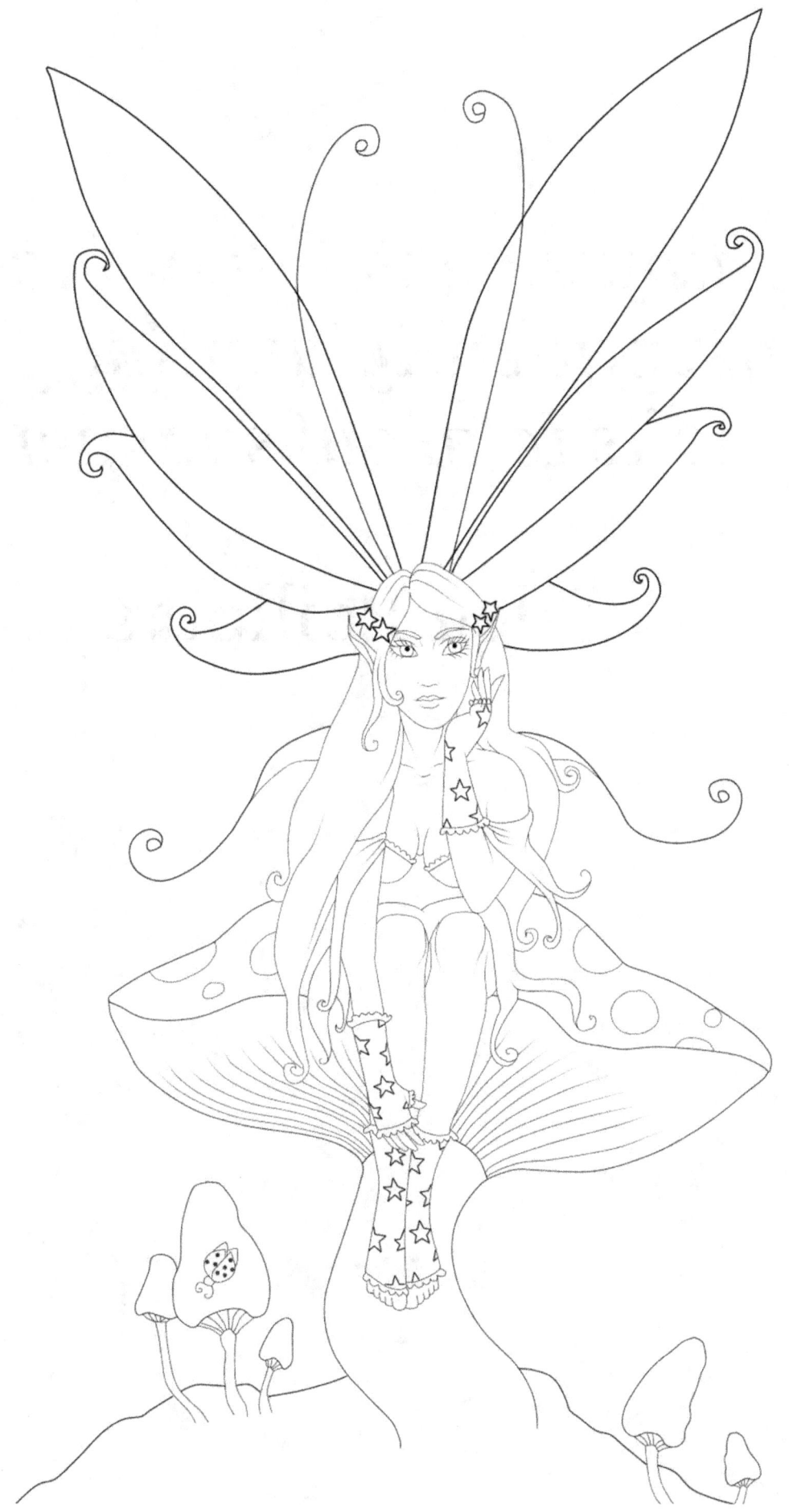

The universe is full of magical things, patiently waiting for our wits to grow sharper.

Eden Phillpots

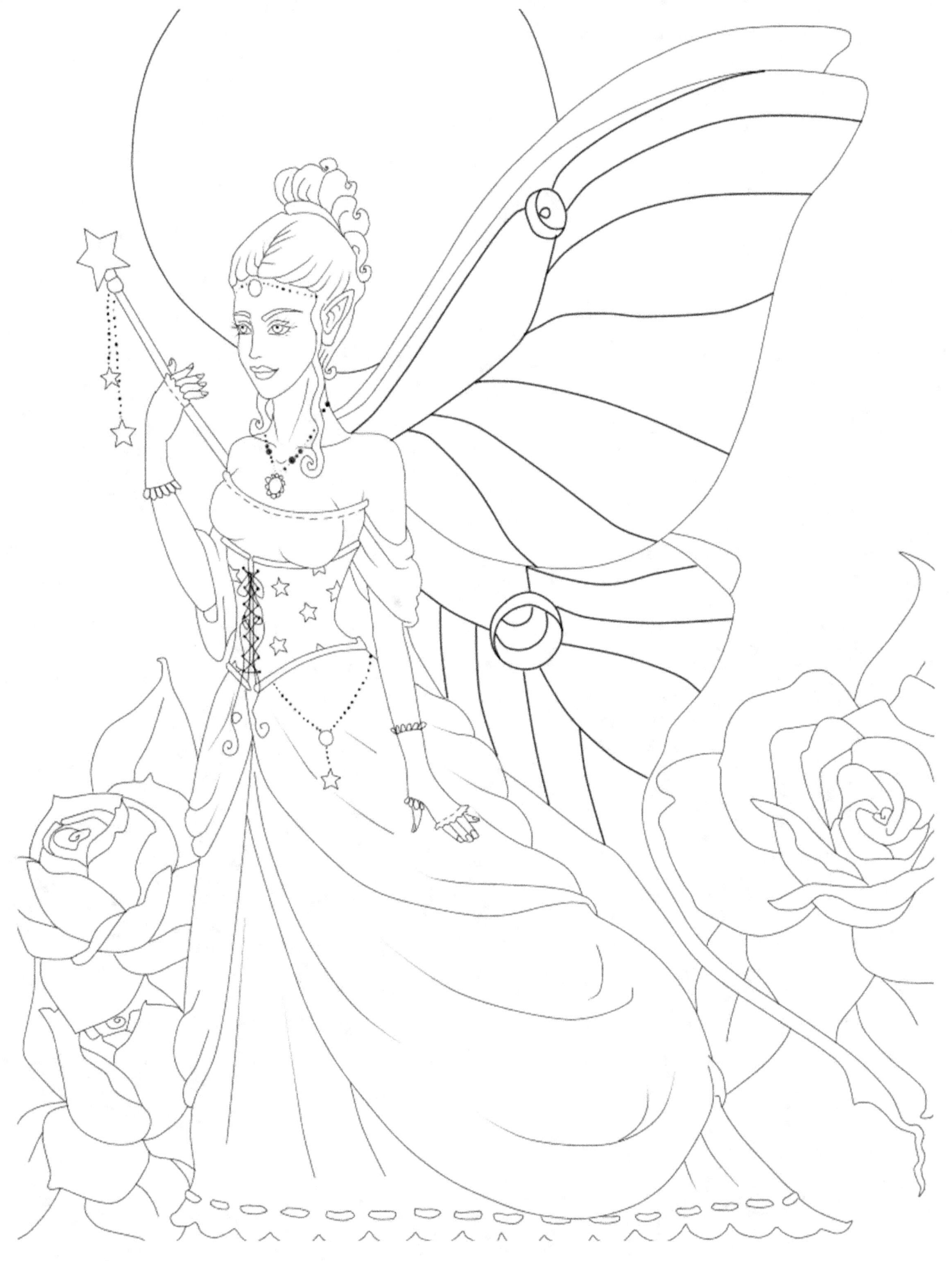

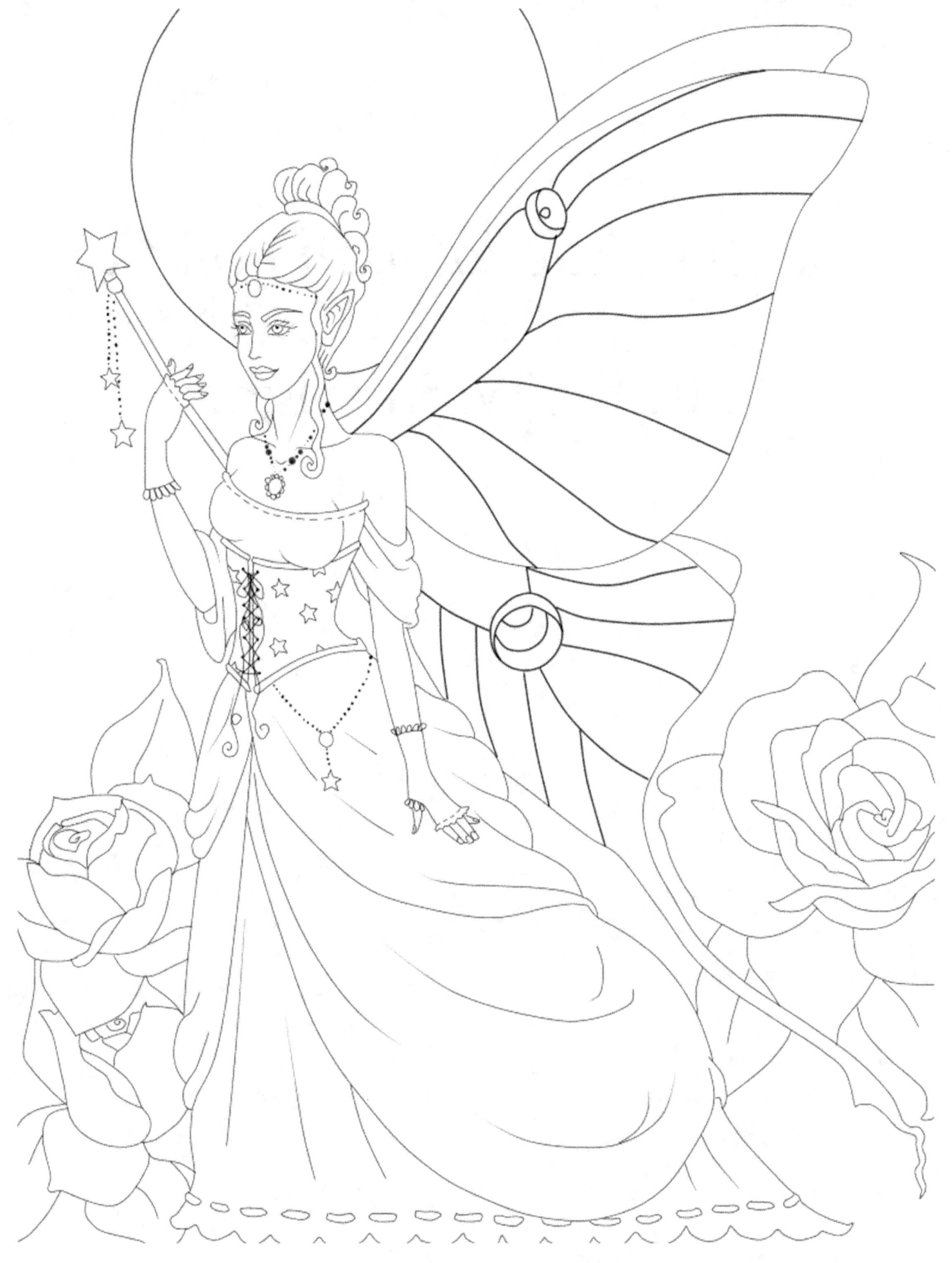

Let the little fairy in you fly!

Rufus Wainwright

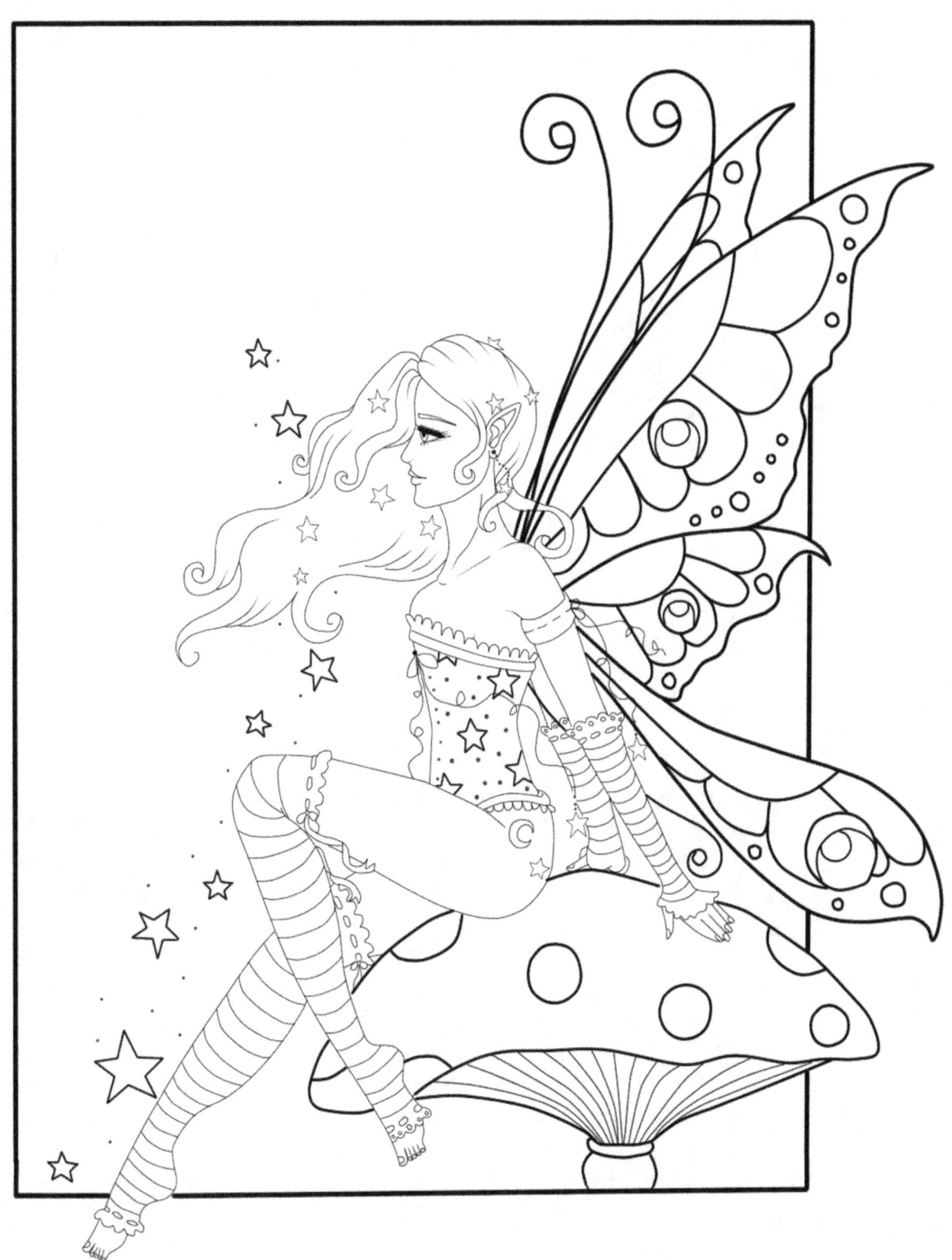

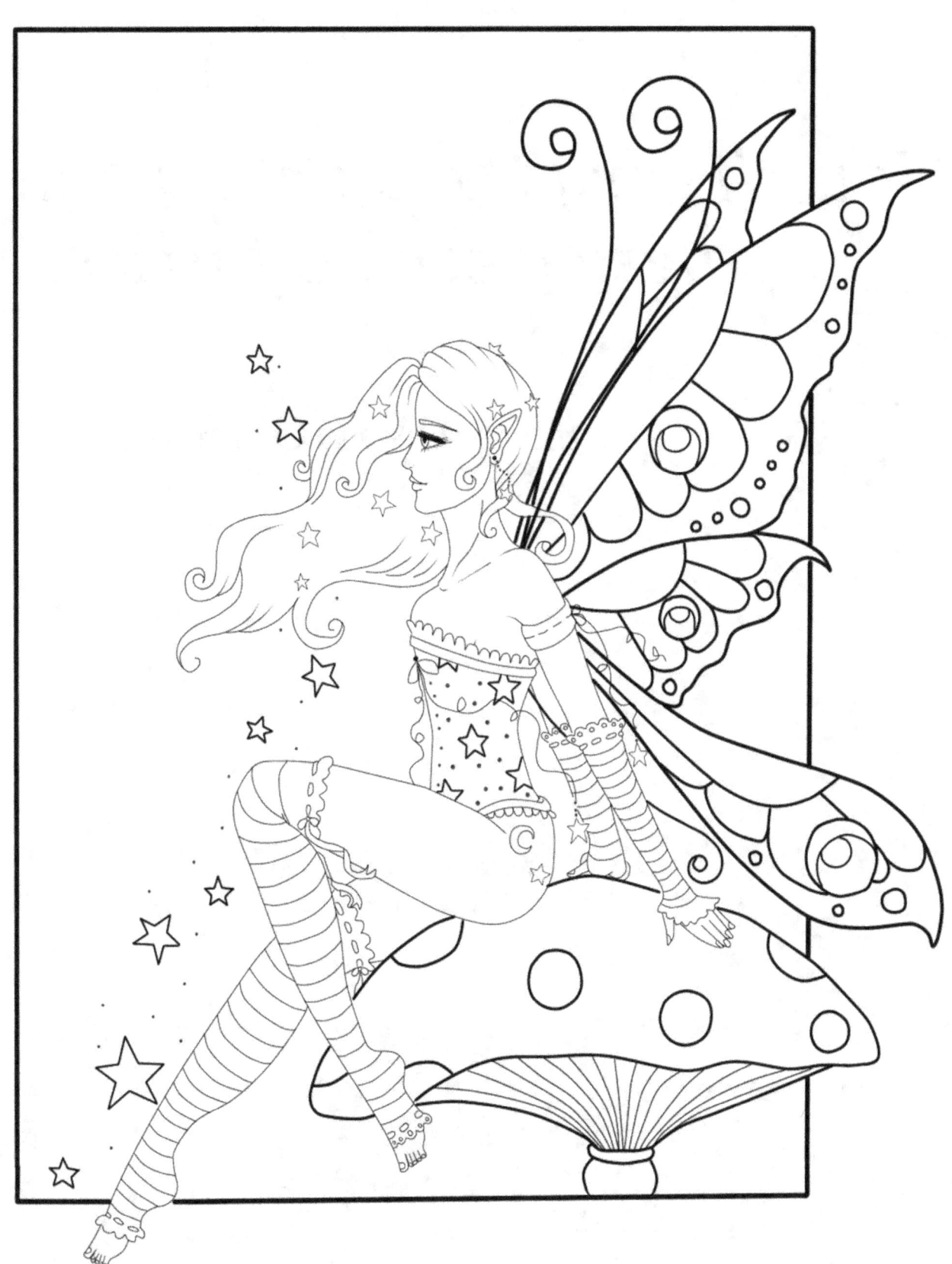

How dreary the world would be if there were no fairies.

Anonymous

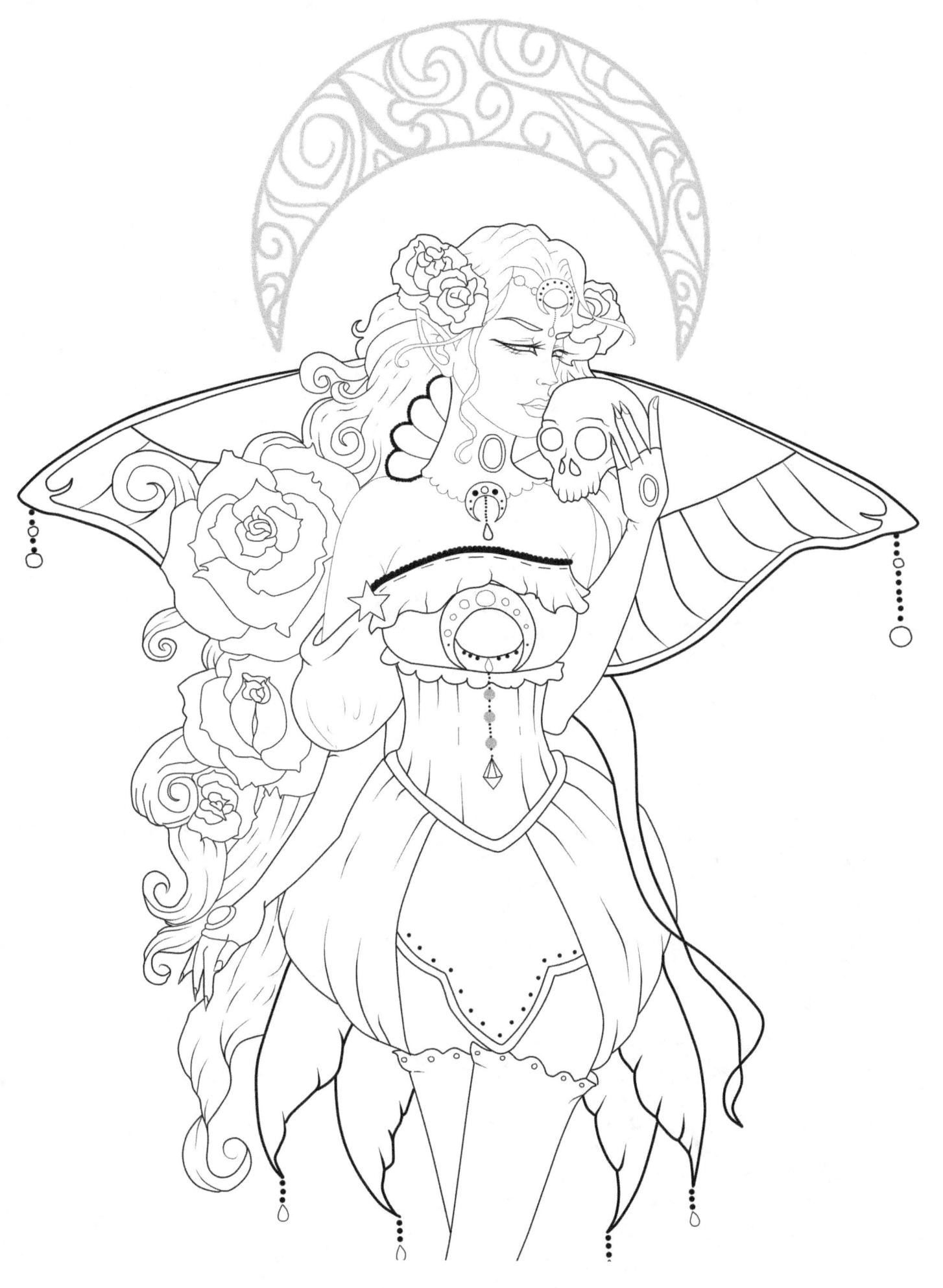

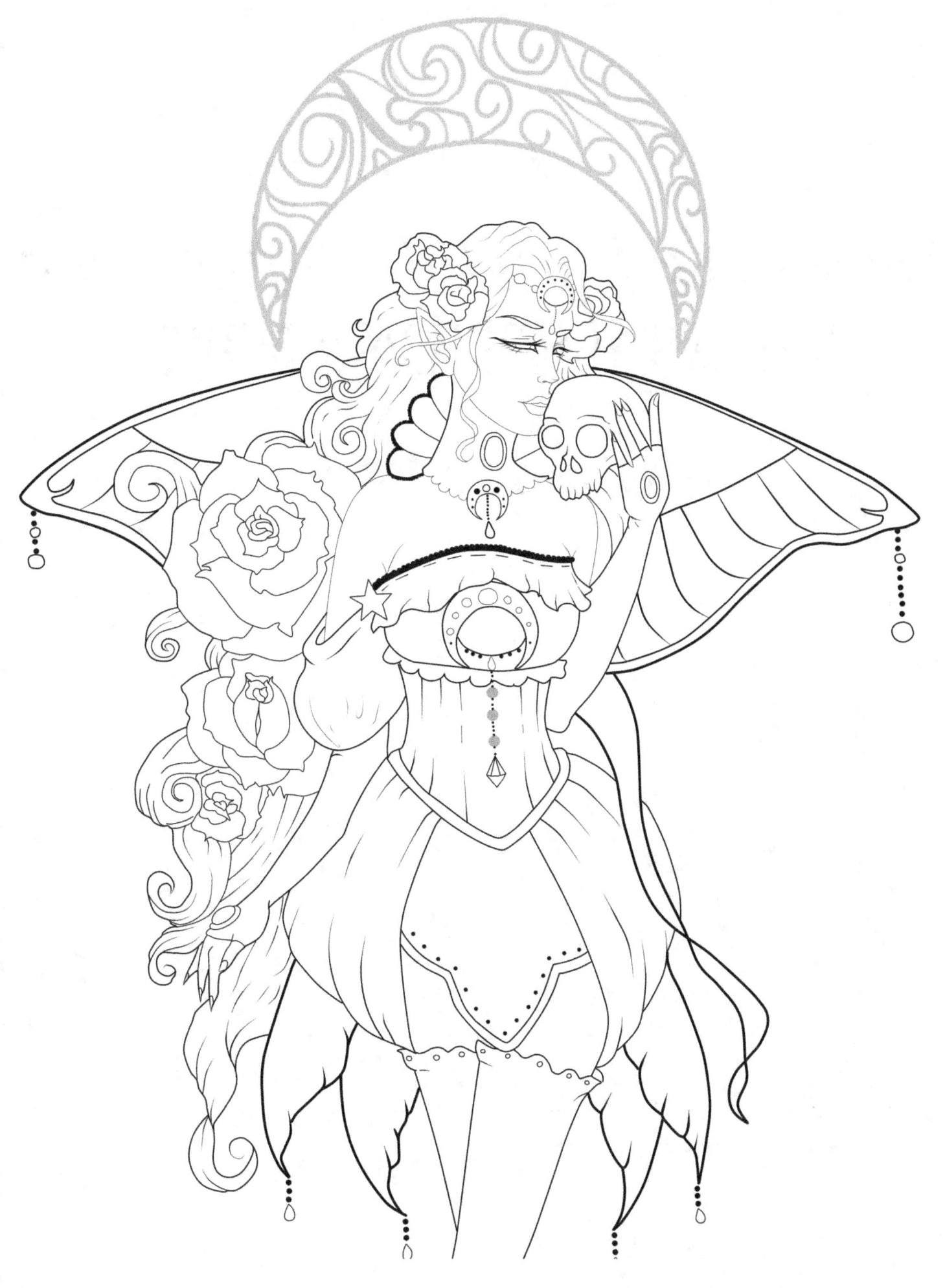

Life is but a fairy tale. But to see it, you must open your eyes.

Olianna Port

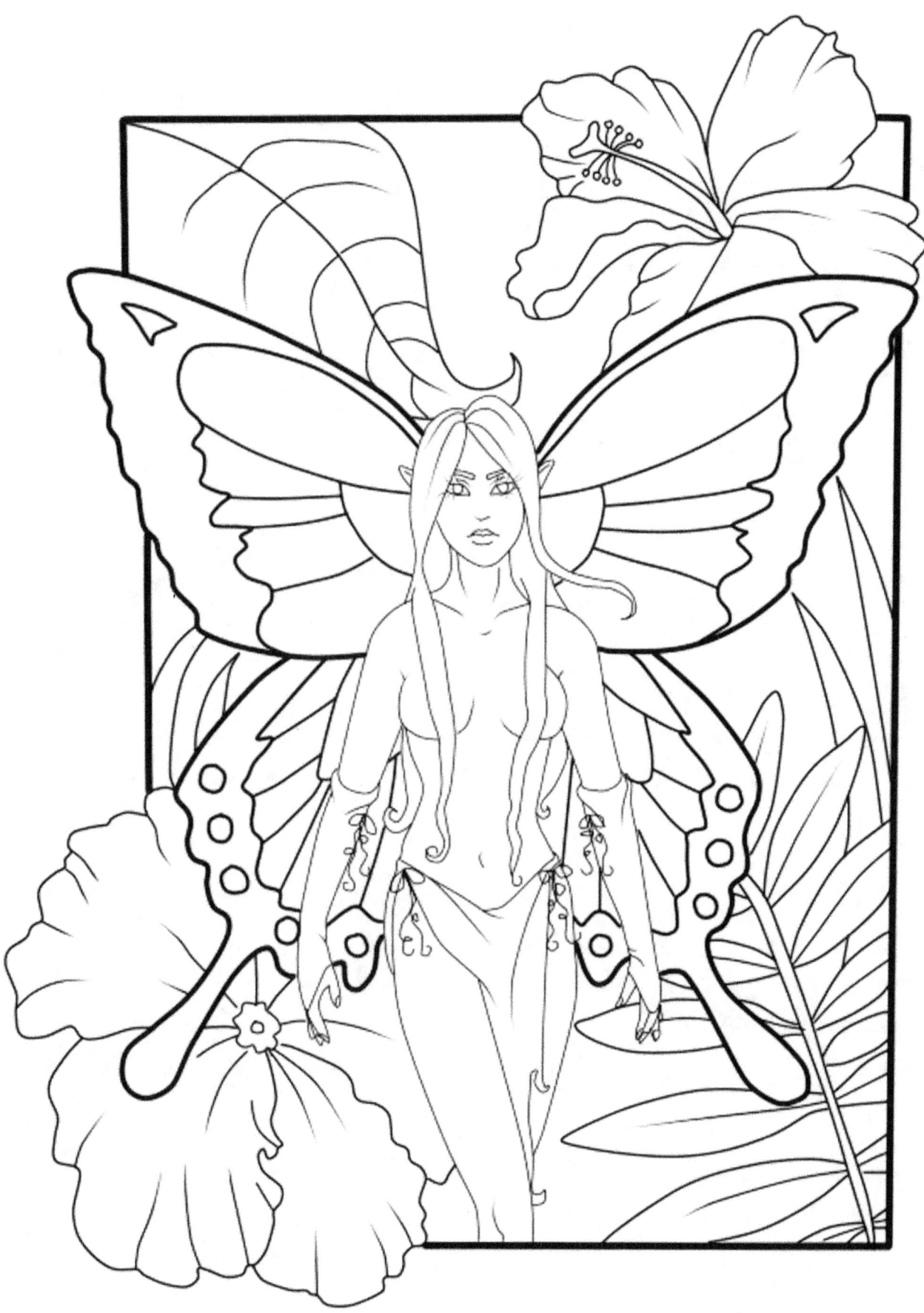

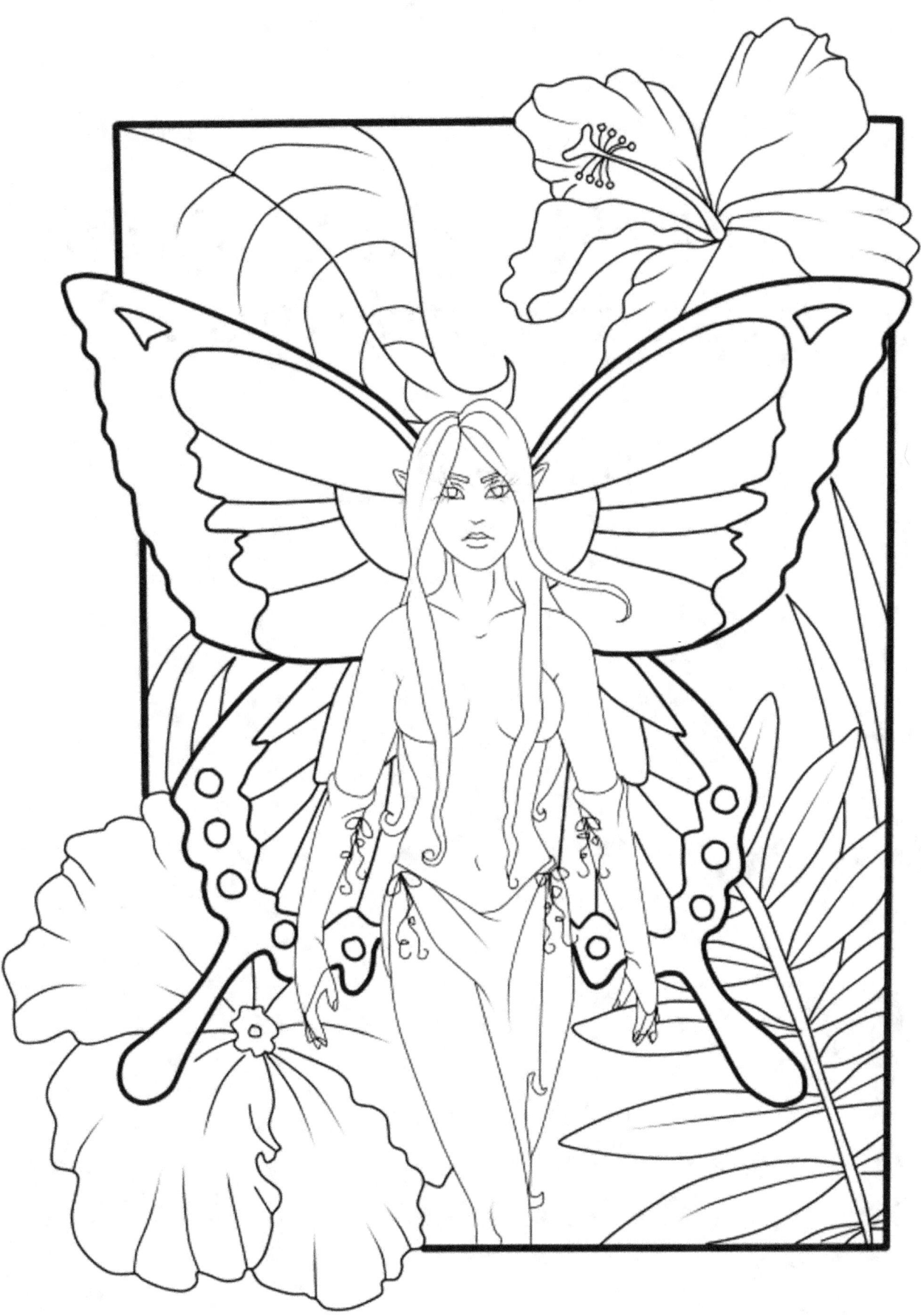

All the world is made of faith,
trust, and pixie dust.

Peter Pan

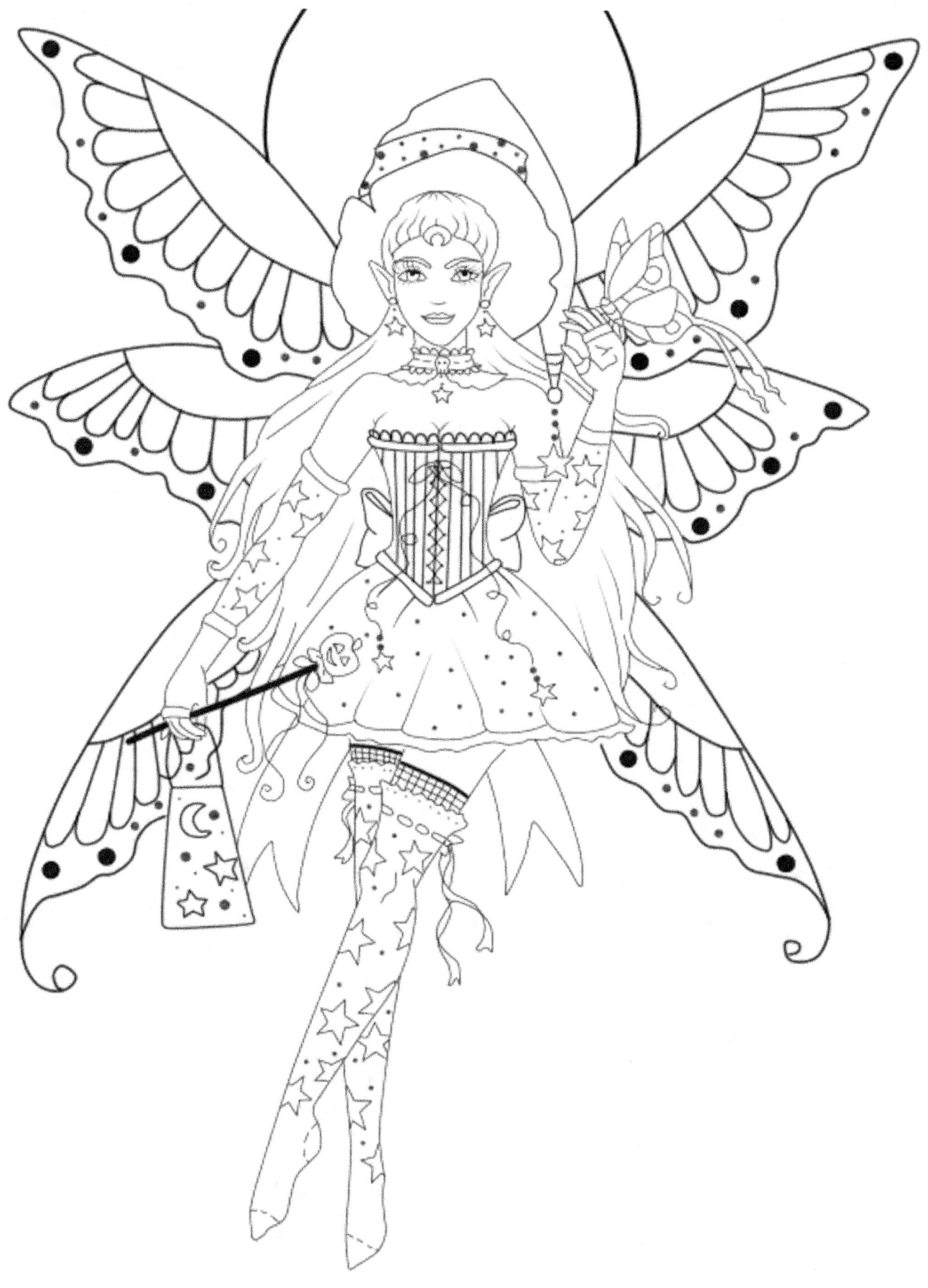

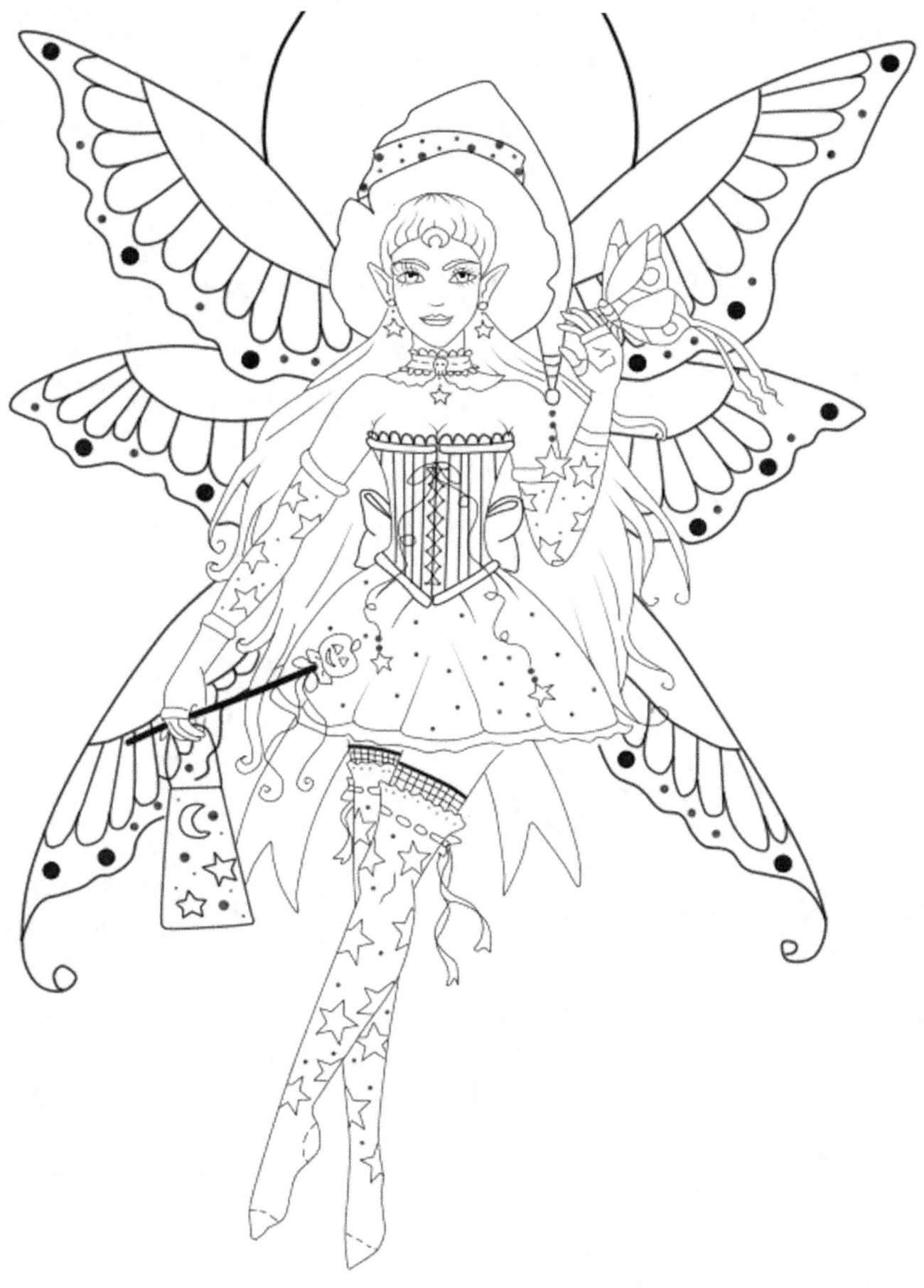

Once upon a time...

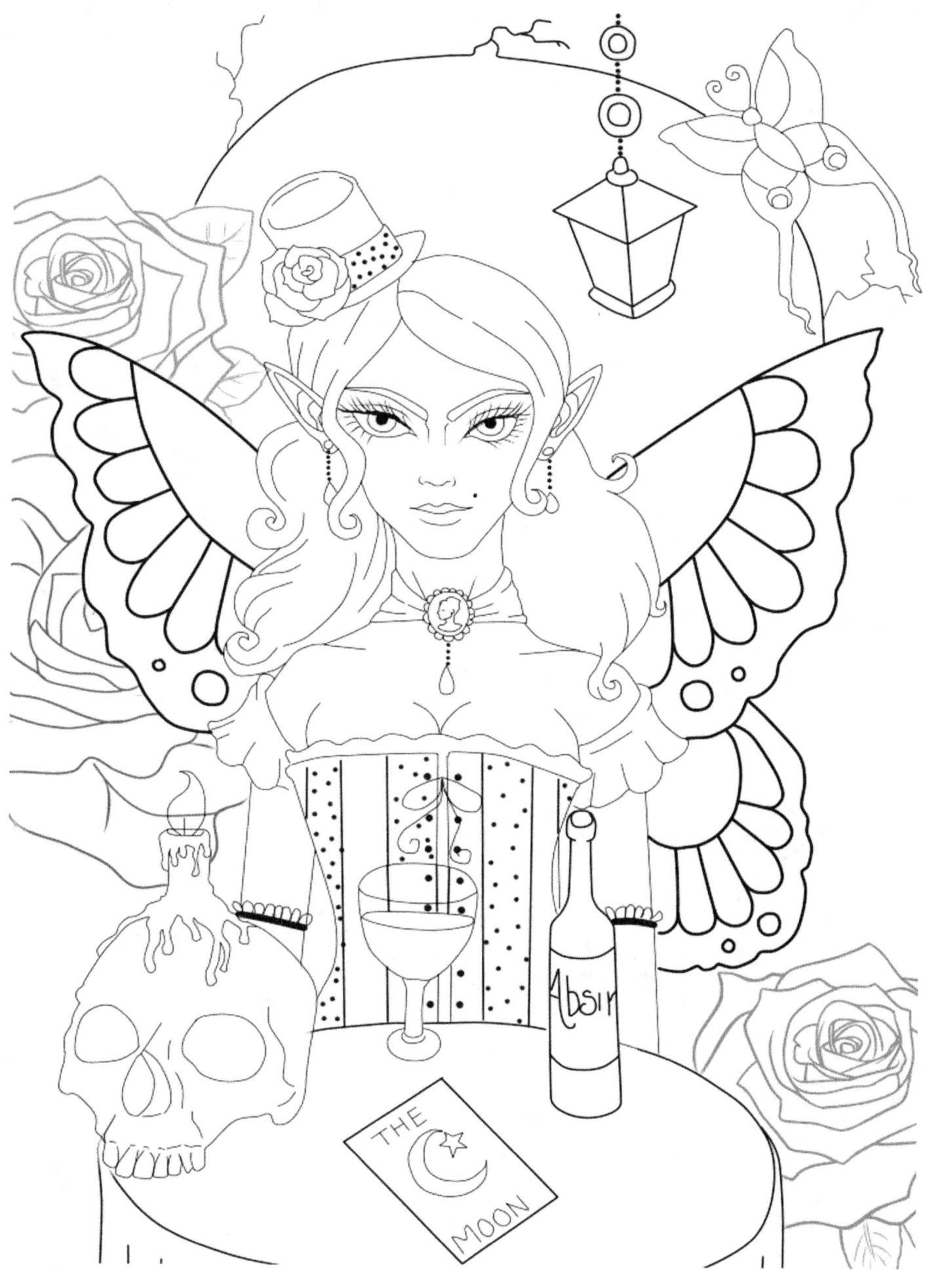

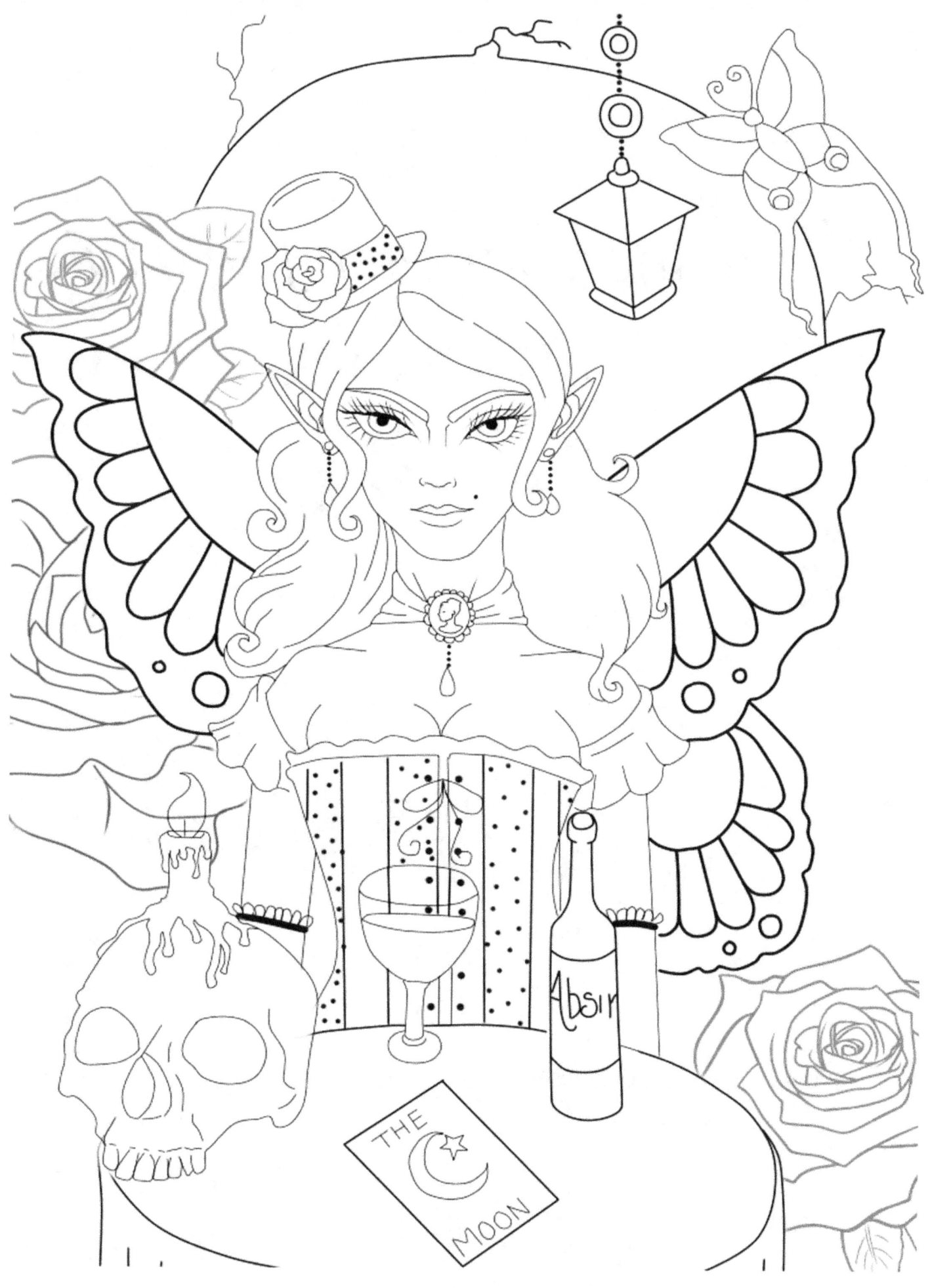

Make life your own fairy tale.

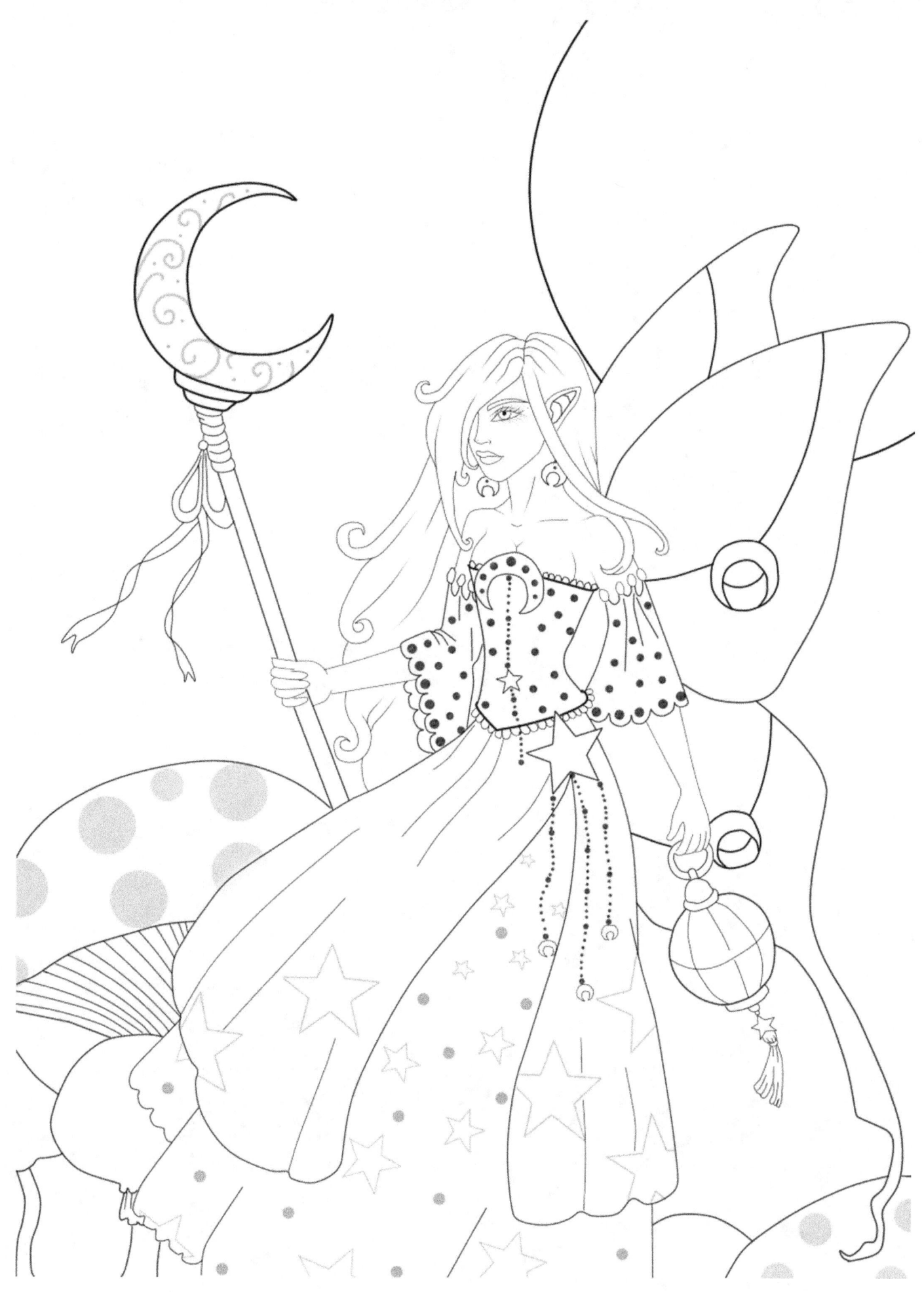

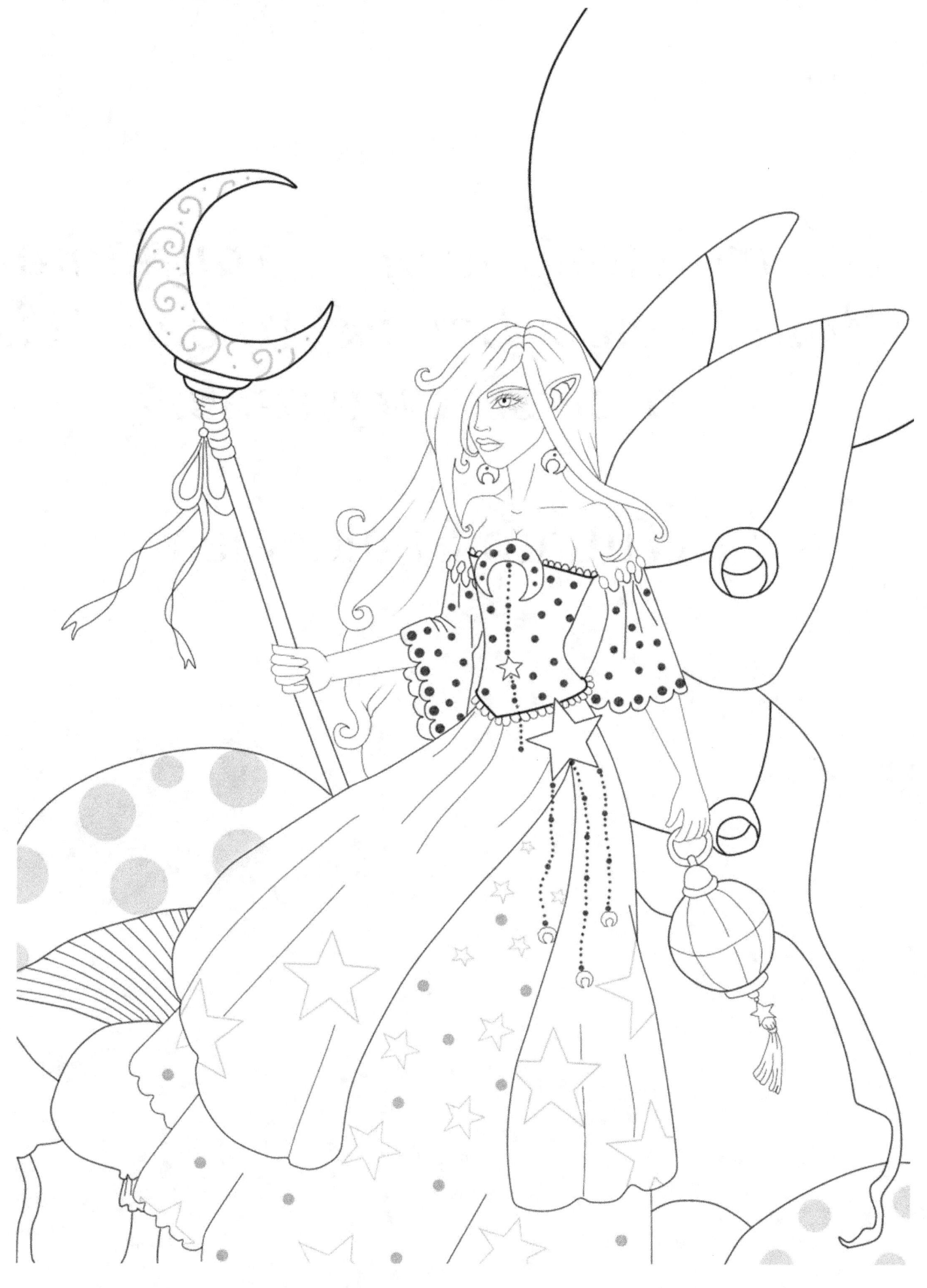

The iron tongue of midnight hath told twelve. Lovers, to bed. 'Tis almost fairy time.

William Shakespear

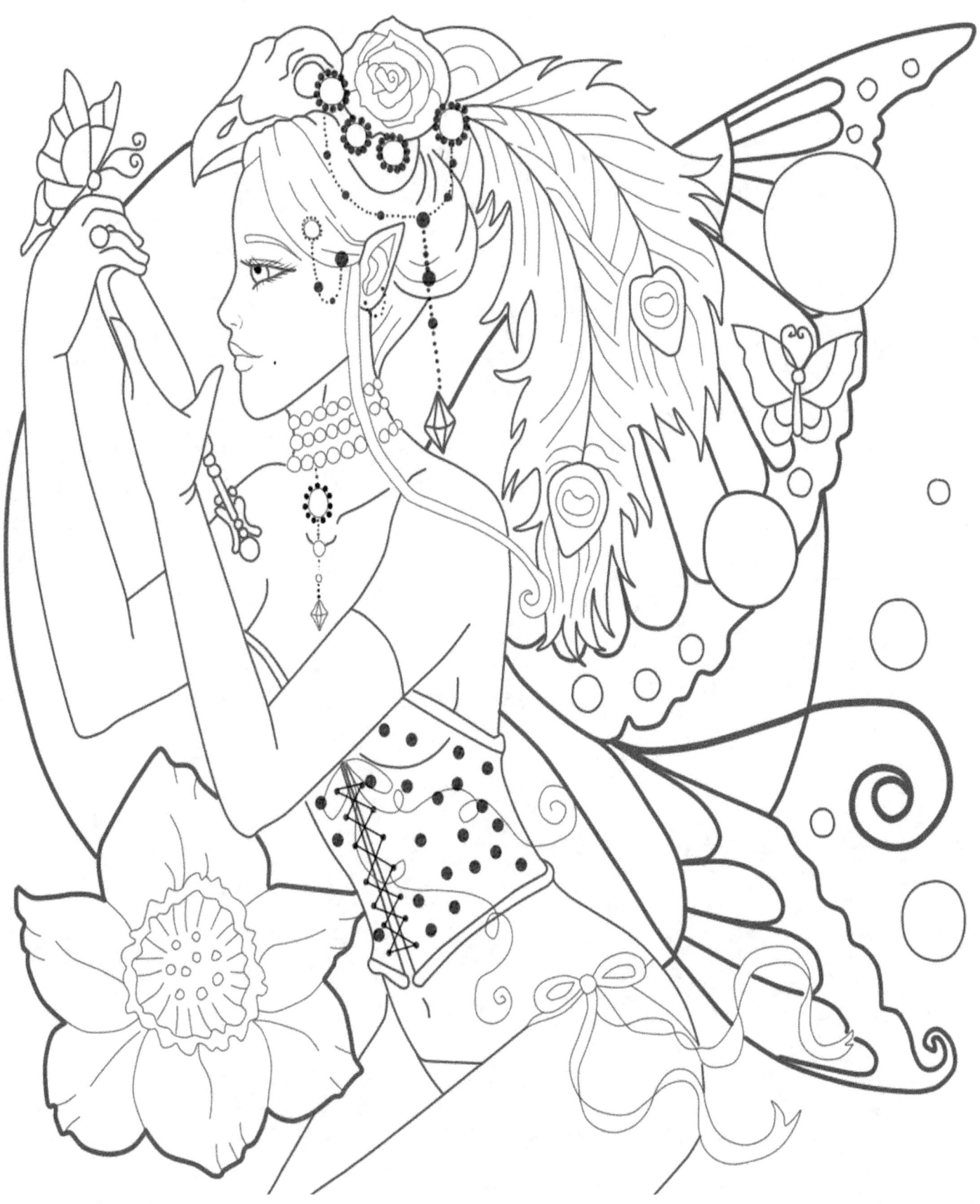

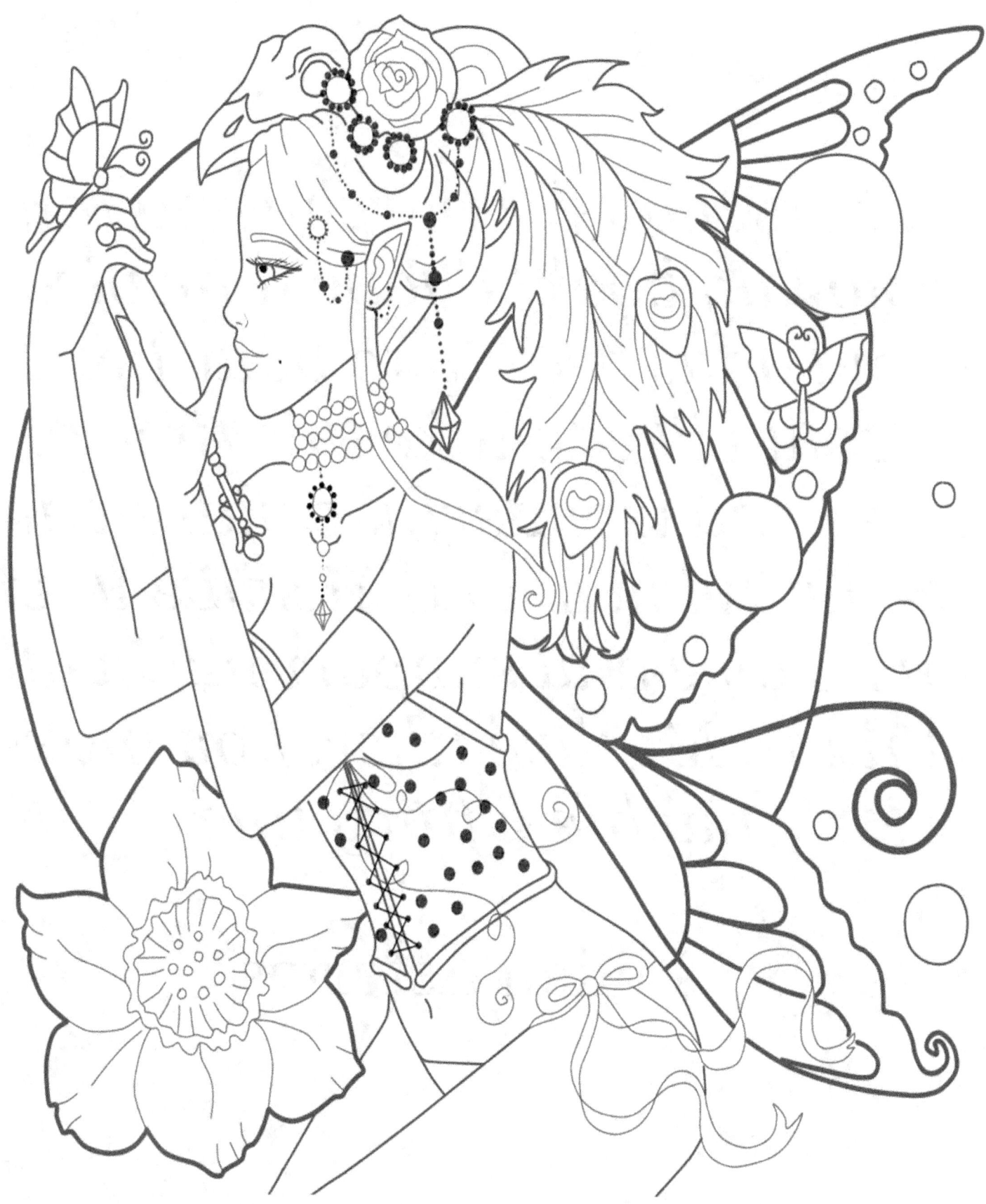

Thank you for purchasing my coloring book. I hope it inspires and adds beauty to your life. I would like to take this time to thank my wonderful children and beautiful husband Meriweather who love and support me in all things. Meriweather, you make my life a fairy tale.

Lillian Asterios

www.ingramcontent.com/pod-product-compliance
Lightning Source LLC
Chambersburg PA
CBHW081208180526
45170CB00006B/2264